THE SKY CLEARS

Poetry of the American Indians

∧∨∧∨∧∨∧∨∧∨∧∨∧∨∧∨∧∨∧∨∧∨∧∨∧∨∧∨∧∨∧∨∧∨∧∨∧∨

by A. GROVE DAY

/\

Verily
The sky clears
When my Midé drum
Sounds for me.

THE
Sky Clears

/\

POETRY OF THE
AMERICAN INDIANS

UNIVERSITY OF NEBRASKA PRESS · Lincoln

Copyright 1951 by A. Grove Day
Library of Congress catalog card number 51-347
Manufactured in the United States of America
International Standard Book Number 0–8032–5047–9

First Bison Book printing March, 1964

Most recent printing shown by first digit below:

9   10   11   12   13   14   15   16   17   18

Bison Book edition reprinted from the Macmillan Company 1951 edition
by arrangement with A. Grove Day

Selections from *The Indians' Book*, by Natalie Curtis, copyright 1907 by Natalie Curtis, copyright 1934 by Bridgham Curtis; reprinted by permission of Paul Burlin.

Selection from Vol. 11, *Mythology of All Races*, by Hartley Burr Alexander, copyright 1920 by Marshall Jones Co., reprinted by permission of The Macmillan Company, publishers.

Selections from *Creation Myths of Primitive America*, by Jeremiah Curtin, copyright 1898 by Jeremiah Curtin, reprinted by permission of Jeremiah Curtin Cardell.

"Darkness Song" by Harriet M. Converse reprinted by permission of New York State Museum.

Selection by John Reade reprinted by permission of the Royal Society of Canada.

Selections from *Journal of American Folk-Lore* copyrighted and reprinted by permission.

Selection from *The Cheyenne Indians*, by George Bird Grinnell, copyright 1923 by Yale University Press, reprinted by permission of the publisher, Yale University Press.

Selections by Frances Densmore reprinted by permission of Southwest Museum and Miss Densmore.

Selections from *Songs of the Tewa*, by Herbert J. Spinden, copyright 1933 by Herbert Joseph Spinden, reprinted by permission of Dr. Spinden.

Selections from *Navajo Creation Myth*, by Hasteen Klah, copyright 1942 by Museum of Navajo Ceremonial Art and reprinted by permission of the Museum.

Selections from *Sitting Bull*, by Stanley Vestal, copyright 1932 by Walter Stanley Campbell, reprinted by permission of Houghton Mifflin Company.

Selections by Frank G. Speck reprinted by permission of University of Pennsylvania Museum.

Selections from *American Anthropologist* reprinted by permission.

Selections from publications of American Museum of Natural History reprinted by permission.

Selection from *Field Museum Anthropological Series* reprinted by permission of Chicago Natural History Museum.

For

YVOR WINTERS Singer of Power

FOREWORD

> Even among the most barbarous and simple
> Indians where no writing is, yet have they their
> Poets, who make and sing songs which they
> call *Areytos*, both of theyr Auncestors deedes,
> and praise of theyr Gods.
>
> PHILIP SIDNEY, *Apology for Poetrie*

LINGUISTS have been occupied for almost a century in the transla-
tion of American Indian poetry into the English language. A
large body of material of this sort may be collected by a diligent ex-
amination of several hundred scattered publications. The transla-
tions which best express the ideas, feelings, and artistic skill of the
Indian originals and which have been put into fitting literary form
deserve study, in their own right, as a part of American literature.
This subject, however, has received almost no attention from the
historians of our literature. This book is designed to present to the
general reader a discussion of the best extant translations of poems
from the North American Indians, as worthy contributions to
American literature.

The book is not intended as an essay in the comparative ethnology
of all the North American tribes on the basis of their differences in
poetic techniques. To make such a study at present would be im-
possible even for the professional Americanist. To begin with, when
Columbus came to the New World in 1492, the independent tribes
in the present United States alone were probably more than two
thousand, of which more than three hundred survive. In historic
times there were according to the Powell classification fifty separate
families of Indian speech in this region; many of these languages
show differences at least as great, say, as that between French and
German. Some two hundred and fifty languages and dialects are

still spoken; no human being could expect to be a master of more than a fraction of these. Of all these tribes or linguistic groups, relatively few are represented by recorded verses. Although the amount of recorded Indian poetry is voluminous, much of it was set down for merely antiquarian ends, or as part of anthropological research, or as texts for linguistic study. There has never been any systematic attempt to cover the entire field of Indian poetry in all the tribes. Many tribes have never been studied; others have been studied by only one or two workers. Many groups have changed their tribal range in the period covered by existing poems, so that the effect of environment could not be easily stated. Perhaps, if a large number of examples of Indian verse were collected over the years and studied with care, reliable statistical observations could some day be made on the differences between the poetry of one tribe and another in matters of style, type, mood, and content.

The purpose of the present volume has been quite different. Most Americans who like poetry and who are quite familiar with the verses of other races (such as the Negro) have no idea that we have a number of fine examples of poetic writing which come from the only truly native New World literature we have. The intention here has been to acquaint readers with the first-rate translations of North American Indian poems produced during the past hundred years. These compositions are not only valuable as poetry, but also serve to reveal the mental and emotional capabilities of the Indians; and the best poems, wherever they came from, deserve appreciation in their own right as contributions to American literature.

The Indian has been too often portrayed in literature either in a sentimentalizing mood or in a manner tinged with suspicion and misunderstanding. The further one studies the Indian revealed by the modern ethnologist, the more one realizes that he was neither a noble savage of the romantic Rousseau variety nor a sadistic demon of the woods. He was a man, with human feelings and human failings. Yet his mind often worked in a different way than do our minds. If we are to attain a proper perspective, we can start by attempting to appreciate the capacities and limitations of the Indians as poetic artists. No one who is not familiar with this poetry should presume to make judgments based on his understanding of the "real" Indian.

As few people in the United States are able to understand even one of the numerous Indian languages or dialects, most of us must, if we are to gain any idea of Indian literature, gain it from translations. Through the medium of first-rate translation one may pleasantly obtain an idea of the achievements of Indian authors— for the most part anonymous authors—in the various branches of native American poetry. Some of the problems facing a translator of verse from Indian sources are discussed in the introductory chapter.

Since this is primarily a book to be read for pleasure, a first consideration has been to select those translations which were *literary* rather than *literal*, and which might be offered as fairly finished pieces in English style which keep to the spirit, even if not to the precise word-for-word rendition, of the Indian originals. This requirement does not imply any weakening in quality—actually, literal translations are easier to make. It does rule out translations which were made with no other thought in mind than to render the denotations or factual meanings for scientific purposes, whereas literary translations are concerned as well with the connotations or suggestive qualities of words. The best translations have been made by men and women who were professional students of Indian languages and who were also endowed with poetic powers of their own. No poet without a thorough knowledge of the Indian tongue he is translating, no matter how gifted in original talent, could even enter upon the task. No one should be surprised that the best translators from a literary point of view—Franz Boas, Daniel G. Brinton, Natalie Curtis, Frances Densmore, Alice Cunningham Fletcher, Washington Matthews, Frank Russell, Herbert J. Spinden, and William Thalbitzer—were not professional poets but professional students of Indian lore and Indian life.

All the selections herein given, more than two hundred in number, were taken from about forty North American tribes, and an effort was made to make these widely representative of the various types and styles to be found in extant translations. Revealing material was not excluded, for example, because it happened to come from the Eskimos or the early Aztecs. It is probable that, if all the surviving Indian poetry were considered as a whole, the similarities in poetic purposes and treatments among the various tribes would be judged more important than the differences. Healing songs, for instance, are quite comparable in their basic ideas wherever in the continent they are found. This is not to say, however, that there are no marked differences in literary achievement and style among the various tribes. Such a false idea is easily controverted by a scrutiny of the various pieces of tribal verse hereinafter given.

In making any general comparative statements, I have kept in mind the fact that the specimens previously translated may not comprise all possible sorts of poetry that might have been found among the Indians in the past. The heavier representation of certain tribes—such, for instance, as those in the southwestern United States —may be due not only to their talent and energy in composition, but also to their availability for study by translators, to the fact that bilingual Indians were ready to assist in interpretation of rituals still carried on in the tribe, and to the particular circumstances of accident or attraction which led a translator to interest himself in the literature of a particular lingual group. It is probable, for example, that the Algonkian tribes of the eastern regions had poetry no less rich than that preserved among the Pueblo groups; but as few of the eastern specimens have survived the long period of decline and decay resulting from the intrusion of white settlers, we can only guess what this "lost" literature might have been.* Moreover, the difficulties of obtaining reliable material of the ritual sort—a sort of poetry in which the Indians were very prolific—are great; most rituals are religious or magical and are therefore secret and treasured possessions of individuals or tribal societies, and many Indians believe that the value of such verses is lost if they become common property. For these reasons, conclusions must be taken to apply only to the body of surviving poetry. This limitation, however, is unavoidable in any examination of early literature (our judgments

---

* Frances Densmore reported in 1943 that the old songs of the Chitimachas of Louisiana had been lost forever because of the recent decline of this tribe.

of ancient Greek or Old English poetry, for instance, rest merely upon our study of surviving specimens), and should not invalidate conclusions if this limitation is kept in mind.

Since the poems for inclusion here were chosen with the intention of seeking the finest translations from the point of view of a modern reader of poetry, it is quite likely that they do not always represent the average or typical songs that for ages have appealed to the Indian himself. Indeed, many Indian songs, literally translated, would strike our sophisticated ears as intolerably dull and long-winded. We do not share the simple delight in repetition which pleases a tribesman with plenty of time on his hands. Nor do we share the understanding of allusions or symbolic phrases which mean much to the initiate. As a typical slice of Indian ritualistic verse one might recommend the voluminous translations of Francis La Flesche from the Osage, where the slight idea content of the songs suffices for days and weeks of tribal singing. The purpose in this book is to show the variety and excellence of many kinds of authentic Indian poetry, and to present those poems which we today can best appreciate. If the thought and expression of these selections are not completely alien to the modern reader, so much the better for the modern reader!

Most Indian poems are not immediately comprehensible to the ordinary person today, however, and this fact has dictated the need for some explanation if a verse is to seem intelligible and pleasing. A mere "anthology" of Indian verse without any clues to the backgrounds of human needs and human emotions from which these unusual poems sprang would be worse than useless, for it would be misleading. There is no use giving the words of a ritual rain-making ceremony unless the reader is first made aware of the desperate importance of rainfall to the Indians of a desert area. Such commentary as seems necessary to set the stage for an aboriginal poem and suggest the impulses which prompted its maker precedes the various selections.

Probably the most important influence upon poetic motives of the Indians—more important than linguistic relationships or traditional borrowings—is culture environment. For this reason, the selections have been grouped in chapters representing "culture areas." This kind of classification of social groups by similarities in culture—the acquirements that make neighboring tribes resemble each other—is coming into increasing use among sociologists. The later chapters therefore present samples of Indian poetry in the various culture areas. The classification of areas closely follows that of Kroeber,[134] except that his "Intermediate and Intermountain" area was not represented, and also his large class of "East and North" was divided into two classes: "Plains" and "Eastern Woodlands."

Titles, for convenience in identification, have been assigned to selections in these chapters to which no titles were given by translators.

The task of discovering the published studies of native poetry has not been simple, and it is hoped that the extensive "Bibliography on North American Indian Poetry" at the end of this book, which indicates all discoverable sources on translations of Indian verse, will be of value to future students in this widely scattered field of research. References to the items in the bibliography are made by superior figures in the text.

This volume is the outgrowth of a dissertation prepared at Stanford University for the degree of Doctor of Philosophy. I wish to acknowledge the advice and criticism given by Dr. Arthur Yvor Winters of the Department of English, who suggested the subject and supervised the early research. I am grateful to the donors of the George Loomis Fellowship in American Literature at Stanford University, under which fellowship research was carried on during two years. Research time has also been granted by the Research Committee of the University of Hawaii. I wish to express thanks for the courtesy of translators and publishers who have freely given permission to reprint selections from printed material.

A. G. D.

University of Hawaii
June, 1950

CONTENTS

≷ 1 ≷

NORTH AMERICAN INDIAN POETRY

THE POEMS of the North American Indians—songs and chants composed by the Indians themselves, which have been translated into English by experts—can seldom be fully appreciated unless the reader has some understanding of the origins of this native verse and the human needs and desires that brought it into being. The aim of this introductory chapter is to answer questions which are bound to arise when one first becomes acquainted with Indian poetry. Just what is Indian poetry? What are the various types of verse found? Who among the Indians compose poetry? What are the sources of Indian poems? What alien influences have affected the native verse? What are the chief problems that the translator must face? How successful are the best translations? What has been the history of the study of Indian poetry?

POETRY WITH A PURPOSE

Poetry composed by American Indians as a part of tribal life grew out of the use of song, and few examples of Indian verse may be found which did not originally serve as the words to a religious or secular song, chant, or recitative.

Song among the Indians was seldom used for mere entertainment or for voicing the soul-cry of an impassioned individualist. Its function, for the Indian, was always quite definite, and was frequently associated with religious or magical ends, to obtain power over invisible life forces. Among the Indians this power brought control over the good creative principle in the world which the Indian needed if he was to achieve anything beyond his individual human strength. As one Indian said, "If a man is to do something more than human, he must have more than human power." [54] Song was a way of tapping this superhuman force, and was used to obtain success in almost every act of Indian life. Songs were the most important instruments of the medicine men, corresponding to our priests and physicians, but any person could by means of dreams and visions find a personal song to help him in time of need.

The best epitome of the function of poetry in the life of the American Indian is given by F. W. Hodge: "Most Indian rituals can be classed as poetry. They always relate to serious subjects and are expressed in dignified language, and the words chosen to clothe the thought generally make rhythm. . . . The picturesque quality of Indian speech lends itself to poetic conceits and expressions. The few words of a song will, to the Indian, portray a cosmic belief, present the mystery of death, or evoke the memory of joy or grief; to him the terse words project the thought or emotion from the background of his tribal life and experience, and make a song vibrant with poetic meaning. Many of the rites observed among the natives from the Arctic Ocean to the Gulf of Mexico are highly poetic in their significance, symbolism, and ceremonial movements; the rituals and accompanying acts, the songs whose rhythm is accentuated by the waving of feathered emblems, the postures and marches, and the altar decorations combine to make up dramas of deep significance, replete with poetic thought and expression." [121]

The poetic impulse was often so strong among the Indians that it carried over into what would ordinarily be classed as prose types. Expressive language—figurative or connotative terms, as well as phrases charged with emotion and fancy—is found in the names of the Indians, and in their orations, chronicles, religious myths, folk

tales, and hero stories. These latter types are not included in the
present volume, which is confined to the particular kind of composi-
tion commonly called poetry.

It is not always easy to state whether a given bit of Indian litera-
ture is prose or poetry. Although the Indians have words for "song"
or "tale," general distinctions are made in few of their languages
between "prose" and "poetry." Owing, however, to the strong con-
ceptions of the Indians concerning the special functions of poetic
forms, there is a sharper demarcation between prose and poetry in
their literature than can be found in European literature, for instance,
where samples of poetic prose (and prosaic verse) are not uncom-
mon. Again Hodge can help to make the point clear: "Prose rituals
are always intoned, and the delivery brings out the rhythmic charac-
ter of the composition. Rituals that are sung differ from those that are
intoned in that the words, in order to conform to the music, are
drawn out by vowel prolongations. If the music is in the form of a
chant, but little adjustment is required beyond the doubling or pro-
longation of vowels; but if the music is in the form of the song, the
treatment of the words is more complex; the musical phrase will
determine the length of a line, and the number of musical phrases in
the song the number of lines to the stanza. To meet the requirements
of the musical phrase the vowels in some of the words will be pro-
longed or doubled, or vocables will be added to bring the line to
the measure required by the music. In many instances similar or
rhyming vocables are placed at the close of recurring musical phrases.
This device seems to indicate a desire to have the word sound recur
with the repetition of the same musical phrase, affording an interest-
ing suggestion as to one of the possible ways in which metric verse
arose. Where vocables are added to fill out the measure of a line,
or are exclusively used in the singing of a phrase or a song, they
are regarded as being unchangeable as words, and no liberties are
ever taken with them.

"The same treatment of words in their relation to the musical
phrase is observed in the secular songs of tribes. In those sung by the
various societies at their gatherings, or those which accompany the
vocations of men or women in love songs, war songs, hunting songs,

or mystery songs, the musical phrase in every instance fixes the rhythm and measure, and the words and vocables are made to conform to it. In many of these songs the words are few, but they have been carefully chosen with reference to their capability of conveying the thought of the composer in a manner that, to the native's mind, will be poetic, not prosaic." [121]

This passage suggests the qualities that distinguish Indian poetry from Indian prose. Poetry was used only on certain occasions; it was always rhythmic in form, and was chanted or sung, usually to the accompaniment of drums or melodic instruments; and the composers made use of certain stylistic devices recognized as poetic—usually consisting of archaic, tersely suggestive, or imaginative language.

TYPES OF INDIAN POETRY

It is probably impossible to invent a logical scheme by which to classify Indian poetry so that it might be easily compared with types of poems common in Old World literature.

It would be absurd, of course, to seek among the Indians for types of form or style; the epic, sonnet, ode, pastoral, metrical romance, and rondeau have grown from certain European conventions that one would not expect to see duplicated in the New World. When we think of the *purposes* for which poetry has always been composed, however, we find that among the Indians—who seldom invented songs without some strong purpose clearly in mind—the mainsprings of poetry are not so very much different from those found in other races.

The Indians made poems for many reasons: to praise their gods and ask their help in life; to speak to the gods through dramatic performances at seasonal celebrations or initiations or other rites; to work magical cures or enlist supernatural aid in hunting, plantgrowing, or horsebreeding; to hymn the praises of the gods or pray to them; to chronicle tribal history; to explain the origins of the world; to teach right conduct; to mourn the dead; to arouse warlike feelings; to compel love; to arouse laughter; to ridicule a rival or bewitch an enemy; to praise famous men; to communicate the poet's private experience; to mark the beauties of nature; to boast of one's personal greatness; to record a vision scene; to characterize the actors in a folk tale; to quiet children; to lighten the burdens of work; to brighten up tribal games; and, sometimes, to express simple joy and a spirit of fun.

The Indians themselves seem to have named some types of verse according to subject-matter, or occasions on which poems were presented, or purposes for which they were composed.

The Abbé Clavigero, for instance, stated that the themes of the ancient Aztecs were various; some poems praised the gods or petitioned them for favors, others recalled the histories of earlier generations, others sought to teach correct habits of life, and others in lighter vein told of hunting, games, and love. Different subjects were chosen for songs used at festivals in keeping with the different seasons of the year. Brinton [23] lists terms for the classes of Aztec songs mentioned by various writers. These are, literally translated: "a straight and true song," direct in expression, used to open a festival; "a song of the spring," figuratively referring to the beginnings of things—the prophetic songs of Nezahualcoyotl were so named; "eagle songs," celebrating famous persons; "flower songs," praising the beauties of flowers; "songs of destitution or compassion"; "songs of the dead"; and other types with geographical names indicating the origins of borrowed tunes or treatments.

The various types of song found for study in a single tribe are here listed from a monograph by Frances Densmore [57] on Chippewa music: Grand Medicine (Midé) songs; dream songs; war songs; love songs; moccasin-game songs; woman's-dance songs; begging-dance songs; pipe-dance songs; songs connected with gifts; songs for the entertainment of children; and a miscellaneous section including "songs of the southern dance, the divorce ceremony, the friendly visit of one band to another, and a song concerning an historical incident."

The principal groups of songs of the Pima tribe are listed thus by Frank Russell: [172] "emergence songs," archaic in diction, telling the myths of tribal origin; festal songs; game songs; hunting songs, some of which had been turned also to the treatment of disease; many medicine songs, for every conceivable ailment; songs for the puberty ceremony; rain songs; and many war songs.

The main purpose of poetry among the Indians, as has been earlier mentioned, was to get hold of the sources of supernatural power, to trap the universal mystery in a net of magical words. Singing, then, was usually a serious business, approached in a reverent mood, and even among the sophisticated Aztecs was seldom indulged in merely for entertainment. Song, as Miss Fletcher observes, was a medium of communication between man and the unseen. "The invisible voice could reach the invisible power that permeates all nature, animating all natural forms. As success depended upon help from this mysterious power, in every avocation, in every undertaking, and in every ceremonial, the Indian appealed to this power through song. When a man went forth to hunt, that he might secure food and clothing for his family, he sang songs to insure the assistance of the unseen power in capturing the game. In like manner, when he confronted danger and death, he sang that strength might be given him to meet his fate unflinchingly. In gathering the healing herbs and in administering them, song brought the required efficacy. When he planted, he sang, in order that the seed might fructify and the harvest follow. In his sports, in his games, when he wooed and when he mourned, song alike gave zest to pleasure and brought solace to his suffering. In fact, the Indian sang in every experience of life from his cradle to his grave." [94]

It is perhaps impossible to devise a scheme whereby all Indian poems, covering these various purposes, could be classified without overlapping or ambiguity—just as it is perhaps impossible to classify all English poems, for instance, in a hard-and-fast system.

One large grouping might be made of religious versus secular poetry. Most of the poetry translated would fall into the religious category; in some tribes no secular poetry has been recorded. To the Indian, hardly any older poetry is devoid of religious, or at least mystical significance.

One who examines the complete body of translated Indian verse gets the impression that almost all of it consists of hymns, prayers, and liturgical sequences like the tropes of the medieval church. Part of this impression is due to the fact that many studies were made by ethnologists who were on the lookout for songs from tribal ceremonies. One should not therefore conclude that the Indians had no lighter moments, when songs were made "just for fun." Anyone who knows the delightful comic spirit of the Indian when he is in a free and relaxed mood will never picture him as a gloomy celebrant who never enjoyed a happy interlude. The fact that collectors of songs seldom sought to record the lyrics of these lighter moments should not lead to the conclusion that no Indians ever sang in blithe mood. The Indian was a strongly social and sociable being who continually sought the company of his friends and relatives, and at play or on the trail or at a party sang joyous nonsense as homely in its appeal as our "Pop Goes the Weasel" or other hayride favorites (see, for instance, the Creek "Crazy Dance" song in Chapter 6).

Yet the fact remains that the large majority of recorded songs were made for purposes essentially serious. Ritualistic verse is found in rich abundance among the first-rate poems in English translation. These types consist of ceremonial chants, which were performed in a dramatic setting (the best of these are found in the Navaho, Pawnee, Osage, Omaha, and Iroquois tribes); explanations of the cosmos, such as the "emergence songs" of the Navaho and Pima tribes; hymns and prayers (especially the Aztec, Pueblo, and Navaho); magical incantations, charms, and healing songs (found in almost all tribes); mourning songs; and war and peace songs (found in most tribes, and especially interesting among the Aztecs, Cherokees, Sioux, Navahos, and Osages). Even what seem at first to be poems descriptive of the beauties of nature are often found to be connected in the Indian mind with religion and worship. The Aztecs produced several first-rate lyricists, in particular the reflective royal poet Nezahualcoyotl, but the pure lyric is a rare form. Neither is the romantic love song a common type, and with the exception of love-charms to compel affection by magical means, most love songs are late and show the influence of white ideas of proper passion. Vision songs are widely found among the Indians; they are often personal charms composed after fasting, or else spring from cult ceremonies—the trance-inspired songs of the revivalist Ghost Dance Religion are of great interest here.

On the secular side, a few pieces of satirical verse are found in translation. These are limited to the "drum-songs" and flytings of the Eskimos, a few boasting contests from the Northwest Coast, and fragments of Maya prophecies. Cradle-songs and lullabies are found among the natives (especially the Eskimos and the Indians of the Northwest Coast), and a few songs from games have been found which are of poetic value. As has been said, secular songs for parties and social dances are not often preserved in literary form. There is a notable lack in the translation of rhythmic work songs among the Indians comparable to our sea chanteys or Negro labor songs. The most surprising lack, however, which arises from a comparison of European and North American Indian types is in narrative verse. The Indian customarily told his tales and legends in prose, and reserved the poetic style for non-prosaic purposes. Accordingly, no specimens have been found among them which would correspond to the European epic, the ballad, or the verse romance. However, the historical chronicle in rude mnemonic lines is fairly well represented by the "Walam Olum" of the Lenape tribe, and fragments of narrative may be found among translations from the Aztec, Maya, and Quiché tribes. A few ritual chants contain brief passages with narrative value; but usually the Indian, although he occasionally inserted a few lines of song into a folk tale, reserved those rhythmic, melodic, and stylistic devices which to him meant poetry for loftier purposes than tale-telling. Poetry was not a pastime. Poetry was power.

Examples of a number of different types of song may be found in a single tribe, but certain tribes seem to excel in certain types. Further comment on characteristics of various types of Indian verse will be found in later chapters.

A type of verse which often appears in prose tales deserves remark. Within the typical Indian folk tale, bits of verse are often found which resemble the song fragments in European or other folk tales. An inserted poem may be either a characterizing song of one of the figures in the story, or may be a dialog recited or sung. To this sort of interlude Sapir has given the name of "song-recitative."

Boas has stated that the main mark of these interpolations, which are found in all primitive narratives, is repetition. The verses may have mere *rhythmic* repetition (as in our story of the giant who always appears saying: "Fe fi fo fum, I smell the blood of an Englishman"), or they may show *sequential* repetition (as in our "House That Jack Built" verses). As an example of rhythmic repetition with simple variation, Boas cites the following cradle-song of the Kwakiutl Indians of the Northwest Coast:

CRADLE-SONG [21]

When I am a man, then I shall be a hunter, O father!
    Ya ha ha ha.
When I am a man, then I shall be a harpooner, O father!
    Ya ha ha ha.
When I am a man, then I shall be a canoebuilder, O father!
    Ya ha ha ha.
When I am a man, then I shall be a carpenter, O father!
    Ya ha ha ha.
When I am a man, then I shall be an artisan, O father!
    Ya ha ha ha.
That we may not be in want, O father!
    Ya ha ha ha.

As an example of the sequential form he gives, from an Eskimo folk tale about the raven and the geese, the inserted verses:

RAVEN RECITATIVE [21]

Oh, I am drowning, help me!
Oh, now the waters reach my great ankles.
Oh, I am drowning, help me!
Oh, now the waters reach my great knees . . .

and so on through all the parts of the body, up to the eyes. This is not greatly different in scheme from the French-Canadian "Alouette" song often heard today.

Sapir has characterized the "song-recitative" in some detail: "This is the short song found inserted here and there in the body of a myth, generally intended to express some emotion or striking thought of a character. It is generally of a very limited melodic range and very definite rhythmic structure. . . . The text to such a song is very often obscure. Even where it does not consist either entirely or in part of mere burdens, the words are apt to be unusual in grammatical form, archaic, borrowed from a neighboring dialect, difficult to translate, or otherwise out of the ordinary." [173]

The narrative portions of a myth told among the Paiute tribe, he explains, are always recited in a speaking voice, but the conversational passages are either spoken or sung, depending upon which particular mythical character is speaking. Coyote, for instance, regularly speaks in expressive prose, but in one story, on hearing of the death of his brother Wolf, he breaks out in a melancholy recitative. There are as many different styles of recitatives as there are characters, and certain characters always sing in the same style no matter what myth they appear in. An example of the typical song-recitative of the myth-character Rattlesnake is given below. Rattlesnake is being carried by Coyote on the way to help in the war against a personage known as Stone-Clothes. Coyote derides the snake as useless, but the other replies that he can kill the antelope which serves as the watchman for the enemy, Stone-Clothes:

RATTLESNAKE RECITATIVE [173]

> While teasing people, carry me then on your back,
>   carry me then on your back!
> I forsooth am the one, that antelope of his
> Who will slay, that forsooth I say.
> O Coyote, Coyote, Coyote, Coyote!

Four "spirit-songs" from the Wintu tribe of California have been translated by Curtin. These seem to be characterizing songs for spirits in folk tales or in shamanistic ceremonies.

SONGS OF SPIRITS [43]

Lightning

> I bear the sucker-torch to the western tree-ridge.
> Behold me! first born and greatest.

Olelbis (The Creator)

I am the great above.
I tan the black cloud.

Hau (Red Fox)

On the stone ridge east I go.
On the white road I, Hau, crouching go.
I, Hau, whistle on the road of stars.

Polar Star

The circuit of earth which you see,
The scattering of stars in the sky which you see,
All that is the place for my hair.

COMPOSITION OF POEMS BY INDIANS

The names of the makers of most of the surviving poems among the Indians are unknown. The religious songs, in particular, although among the most beautiful, are always anonymous. These rituals were assumed to have been inspired by supernatural beings, and the medicine man of olden times who worked out such a song might have explained, in order to give authority to the words, "The god told me to say this," or "The spirits of the dead have given me this song in a vision." Only a few of the poems given in later chapters have known authors. An exception is the group of songs attributed to an Aztec prince, Nezahualcoyotl. The war songs of Sitting Bull, who was a medicine man as well as a war chief, are also known to be individual compositions.

We know, however, that anyone among the Indians could make songs. Every Indian was a potential poet. Many ceremonies encouraged the invention of personal songs relating experiences either real or seen in visions. It is said that in the old days all the important songs were composed in dreams; these songs were sung in times of danger or need to draw forth the aid of the supernatural power offered in the dream, and thus to bring success in war, in hunting, in healing others, or in any other serious effort. Each member of the

Ghost Dance Religion cult composed a song of what he saw each time he went into a trance at each meeting, so that a single meeting might easily result in twenty or thirty new songs.

Women as well as men were permitted to make verses. This patriotic song by a Sioux woman was translated by Frances Densmore:

YOU MAY GO ON THE WARPATH [54]

You may go on the warpath;
When your name I hear [announced among the victors]
Then I will marry you.

The same translator gives a humorous song obtained from a Papago woman:

I MET A MEXICAN [72]

While I was running I met a Mexican who said,
"How do you do?"
While I was running I met a Mexican with a long beard who said,
"How do you do?"

Alice Fletcher [94] mentions the Wé-ton songs of the Omaha, composed and sung by women for the purpose of extending protection over absent warriors. Several of the Ghost Dance songs given by Mooney were the work of women, as were most of the Chinook songs collected by Boas.

Poems were considered to be the property of certain individuals or groups. Every song had originally an owner: a person, or a clan, or a tribal religious or fraternal society. By a kind of primitive copyright, the privilege of singing a song belonging to an individual could be protected and purchased.

Sometimes each person sang his individual song in competition with other members of a singing group. The resulting bedlam of discord is well sketched by Miss Fletcher: "Certain societies require that each member have a special song; this song is generally of the man's own composition, although sometimes these songs are inherited from a father or a near relative who when living had been a member of the society. These individual songs are distinct from songs used in the ceremonies and regarded as the property of the society, although the members are entitled to sing them on certain occasions. When this society holds its formal meetings, a part of the closing exercises consists of the simultaneous singing by all the members present of their individual songs. The result is most distressing to a listener, but there are no listeners unless by chance an outsider is present, for each singer is absorbed in voicing his own special song which is strictly his own personal affair, so that he pays no attention to his neighbor; consequently the pandemonium to which he contributes does not exist for him." [96]

Indian songs vary in length from a few words to extended ceremonials which might run on for days at a time. Thus, a song in honor of a Chippewa brave consisted of only two words—one meaning "warrior" and the other the name of the hero. The people were supposed to know his valiant deeds and it was not necessary to mention even one of them. In contrast to this two-word poem, the "Night Chant" of the Navaho tribe contains a sequence of no less than 324 different songs which made up one long ritual poem recited over a succession of days and nights.

SOURCES OF INDIAN POETRY

Original Indian songs have been obtained for translation in a number of ways. The ideal method, used today wherever possible, is to record a song on a phonograph so that it can later be interpreted by careful and repeated study, if possible with the aid of the singer himself or a bilingual Indian of the same tribe. The "Hako" ceremony of the Pawnee tribe was thus recorded. This modern method has not long been available, however, and most of the poems appearing in this book were obtained for translation by less objective means.

Many of the earlier songs were written down by missionaries in adaptations of European alphabets. An example of this sort is the Iroquois "Book of Rites," the provenance of which is described in Chapter 6. The Aztec poems translated by Brinton were taken from originals written down shortly after the Conquest of Mexico, when the Nahuatl language had been reduced to the Spanish alphabet; the translator gives the Nahuatl versions on opposing pages.

Rarely, Indians may write down their songs in an Indian alphabet. About the only example of this sort of record is to be found in the Cherokee charms (see Chapter 6), which were handed down orally for generations until the early nineteenth century, when the invention by Chief Sequoya of the celebrated Cherokee alphabet enabled the tribal priests to put them in writing.

Occasionally, an Indian who knows English may write out both original and translation. A good example is the work of Francis La Flesche, who gives the original songs in a roman alphabet.

Most difficult is the interpretation of Indian pictographic records. The various kinds of picture-writing use symbols which should call to memory a line of verse or brief song already learned. The Midé songs of the Chippewa tribe were transcribed, with the aid of the singers themselves, from ideographs carved on birch-bark scrolls in the possession of this medicine society. The "Walam Olum" chronicle of the Lenape Indians (see Chapter 6) is a rhythmic recitative based upon pictographs which, although merely crude sketches engraved on wood, have high mnemonic value. The provenance of the "Walam Olum" will be described further when this poem is given in full.

Frances Densmore, who studied the songs of many tribes, frequently depended upon educated native interpreters with good results. "The interpreter who translates literally, without paraphrasing or enlarging upon the idea, is the only interpreter whose work is reliable," she has stated. "The words often sound absurd to him, and he is tempted to introduce the phraseology of the missionary, but when this is done the native quality disappears." [54] She credits the government and the mission schools with the fact that trained Indian interpreters can nowadays use English with rare discrimination and render valuable aid in the translation of Indian verse.

ALIEN INTRUSIONS IN INDIAN POETRY

The influence of white culture is occasionally found in certain Indian poems, and is fairly easy to detect by one familiar with authentic tribal verse. Were these alien intrusions not detected, however, or were the reader to be imposed upon by forged poems or hoaxes, he might be entirely too ready to say: "The Indian poets are after all quite like us, aren't they?"

Most of the examples given in later chapters are untinged by alien influences, for the aim has been to get as close to native thinking and expression as possible. The insertion of a Christianized phrase, for instance, stands out strikingly. In the Iroquois "Book of Rites" the line "God has appointed this day" was inserted, probably at the suggestion of the missionaries who transcribed the verses. Sometimes an early poem will use a foreign word to express an Indian idea; in an Aztec poem the original Nahuatl language adopted the Spanish word for God (*Dios*) to designate one of the deities of their native pantheon. A few pre-Conquest poems given by Brinton [23] include Christian-sounding lines which were probably inserted later by the person who wrote them down, "to remove the flavor of heathenism." A complete poem showing Christian use of the poetic form of the ancient Aztecs was prepared shortly after the Conquest, probably by the Mexican bishop Zumárraga, to be sung by the recent native converts. The form is comparable to that of typical Aztec hymns (see Chapter 7), but the thought and phraseology are notably different.

AZTEC HYMN TO THE VIRGIN [23]

Resting amid parti-colored flowers I rejoiced; the many shining flowers came forth, blossomed, burst forth in honor of our mother Holy Mary.

They sang as the beauteous season grew, that I am but a creature of the one only God, a work of his hands that he has made.

Mayst thy soul walk in the light, mayst thou sing in the great book, mayst thou join the dance of the rulers as our father the bishop speaks in the great temple.

God created thee, he caused thee to be born in a flowery place, and this new song to Holy Mary the bishop wrote for thee.

The most common influence of white ideas upon native verse is found in the love songs of the various tribes, most of which are

quite modern. The effect of contact with white men of the North-
west Coast may be amusingly noted in the songs from the Chinook
jargon. These vulgar verses reveal the demoralizing effect of the
loose life of the ports and steamboat docks and beer-houses upon the
Indian breeds of the Pacific shore.

CHINOOK SONG [17]

I don't care
If you desert me.
Many pretty boys are in the town.
Soon I shall take another one.
That is not hard for me!

Another of these verses is in a mixture of languages; the first two
lines are in the Tlingit dialect, the last line in Chinook pidgin:

CHINOOK SAD SONG [17]

Nothing shall bother my mind now.
Don't speak to me. I wish I were dead,
With my sister.

An interesting example of the influence of their romantic Mexican
neighbors upon the belligerent Yaqui tribe of Sonora is given by
Miss Densmore:

TULE LOVE SONG [82]

Many pretty flowers, red, blue, and yellow.
We say to the girls, "Let us go and walk among the flowers."
The wind comes and sways the flowers.
The girls are like that when they dance.
Some are wide-open, large flowers and some are tiny little flowers.
The birds love the sunshine and the starlight.
The flowers smell sweet.
The girls are sweeter than the flowers.

The amorous and sophisticated nature of this song is in strong
contrast to the repetitive simplicity of the typical Yaqui song, of
which this is a good sample:

YAQUI SONG [82]

In summer the rains come and the grass comes up.
That is the time that the deer has new horns.

All foreign intrusions are not confined to love songs. A lullaby of the Pueblo Indians of San Juan which the translator finds strongly comparable to Spanish nursery songs runs as follows:

SAN JUAN LULLABY [87]

La, la, la la, go to sleep, baby!
The *tsabio* [bugaboo], the old *tsabio* will get you.
Be quiet. Go to bed and sleep, my dear little baby.

A translator of Eskimo songs considers the following piece overlaid by the style of European civilization:

SONG FROM SOUTHERN SERMILIK [195]

Oh, that it would fall to rest,
The sea off of Sermilik fjord,
That it would fall to rest!

Oh, that it would brighten,
The deepest recess of Sermilik fjord,
That it would brighten!

Attempts at forgery of Indian songs have been few, because the difficulties are great and the reward trivial. One notorious hoax, however, is a classic reminder that the collector of these songs, like other collectors, must always be on guard.

The following translation was printed in 1883 by D. G. Brinton:

TAENSA MARRIAGE SONG [22]

Tikaens, thou buildest a house, thou bringest thy wife to live in it.
Thou art married, Tikaens, thou art married.
Thou wilt become famous; thy children will name thee among the
    elders. Think of Tikaens as an old man!
By what name is thy bride known? Is she beautiful? Are her eyes
    soft as the light of the moon? Is she a strong woman? Didst thou
    understand her signs during the dance?
I know not whether thou lovest her, Tikaens.
What said the old man, her father, when thou askedst for his pretty
    daughter?
What betrothal presents didst thou give?
Rejoice, Tikaens! be glad, be happy!
Build thyself a happy home.
This is the song of its building!

In 1890, Brinton [26] contritely exposed the spuriousness of this song, which in comparison with authentic Indian poetry has the sentimental and un-Indian ring of romanticized imitations to be found in European literature. He had been imposed upon by a fake. An entire alleged Indian language—grammar, vocabulary, prose, and poetry— had been fabricated by two artful young Frenchmen and published as a hoax played upon the learned world. Despite this exposure by Brinton, the poem was cited in an anthology published in 1918 and reprinted in 1934 as "the faithful translation of an unliterary explorer, Greek in its mode, and in a certain tender irony of mood, but with touches to which only a full knowledge of Indian thought can give their full value." [42] The poem doesn't sound Indian: it may sound Greek; it sounds more like Chateaubriand.

THE TRANSLATION OF INDIAN POETRY

Judgment as to whether an English version is more or less faithful to the letter and spirit of the Indian original is properly a matter for an expert in linguistics. Since all the first-rate translators are specialists in the Indian dialects of the originals, they can presumably be criticized only by their peers in these studies. The problems that beset a translator of Indian verse have often been remarked upon by the translators themselves, however, and their attack upon them should be of interest to anyone who is concerned with the art of recreating the poetic expression of one language through the medium of any other language.

Translation of this Indian material is a difficult but not impossible task. "The peculiarities of Indian language," says Hodge, who is fully qualified to speak, "and the forms in which the Indian has cast his poetic thought, particularly in song, make it impossible to reproduce them literally in a foreign language; nevertheless they can be adequately translated." [121] Despite difficulties, it is possible to translate Indian poetry with the same success to be expected in translating other foreign poetic literature into English.

The particular problems of translating Indian poetry may be briefly discussed under the headings of meaning, style, and meter (rhythm).

MEANING

The proper translation of the meanings of Indian poems is made difficult by the fact that when many songs, chants, or recitatives are taken out of their ceremonial setting, much explanation is required in order that the reader may try to visualize the particular function for which the poem was composed. For this reason, some of the verses later presented would be almost incomprehensible unless accompanied by some description of their ritual or social function, or of the legends of which they were a reflection. The difficulties of rendering literal translations of Indian poetry—especially ritual poetry—are increased by the use of symbolism, figurative language, secret language, archaic language, and allusions to Indian myths and other parts of the Indian background which the hearer was supposed to understand and take for granted.

Symbolism is the key to Indian poetry as well as to Indian graphic art. "The cloud-form in Indian design is no copy of a cloud, but a conventionalized image that is a symbol *meaning* cloud, as a wavy line means water or a cross stands for a star," says Natalie Curtis. "Even so in poetry. One word may be the symbol of a complete idea that, in English, would need a whole sentence for its expression. . . . Such poetry is impressionistic, and many may be the interpretations of the same song given by different singers." [44] The inner meanings of many lines from rituals can be known only by an understanding of tribal symbols.

Figurative language of a metaphorical or allusive sort abounds in Indian poetry and adds to the difficulties of exact translation. Metaphor is not confined to Indian poetry; indeed, much of the strength of their oratory in prose was to be found in the power of arousing emotion by making telling comparisons. It is in poetry, however, that extended metaphor is relied upon most heavily. Fixed metaphors are the outstanding feature of Zuñi poetic style, according to Ruth L. Bunzel.[32] In their prayers, the sun always "comes out standing to his sacred place," "night priests draw their dark curtain," the corn plants "stretch out their hands to all directions calling for rain," the meal painting on an altar is always "our house of massed clouds," prayer sticks are "clothed in our grandfather, turkey's, robe of cloud." In a ritual from the same tribe, to light a cigarette is to take "reed youth," place "mist" (smoke) within his body, and take his "grandmother" (fire) by the hand and make her sit down in the doorway (the end of the cigarette). Delight in deliberate ambiguity or puns is often found. The Indians were not always seeking clarity in meaning, and what might seem to us cloudiness of expression might even be prized for its own sake. The Navaho, according to Washington Matthews,[145] felt no discomfort if a passage in a chant seemed to have two quite different meanings.

Secret language was often used in the songs of religious organizations, so that only the initiate in their mysteries would understand them. Some of the Midé songs of the Chippewa contain esoteric phrases.

Archaic language has been remarked upon by a number of translators. Many words used in songs are not found in the conversational idiom. "In some instances," writes Miss Densmore, "the meaning is known, as a few words of the obsolete language are still in use, but the Yuma recorded many old songs with continuous words whose meaning they did not know. They said they sang the words exactly as they had been taught by the old men, but the meaning of the words was lost forever." [54] Says Matthews: "Many archaic words appear in the songs for which the Navahos have only traditional meanings or none. Many meaningless vocables are introduced for the sake of meter and rhyme and such vocables are as essential, and must be repeated as faithfully, as the most significant words." [145]

Allusions to Indian commonplaces often bring perplexity to the translator and to the modern reader. Many expressions baffling to us would be taken for granted by the Indian listener. The reader must know the myths and customs from which the poetry springs.

Take, for example, these opening lines rendered by Dr. Matthews:

From the doorway with the blue *kethawns*. Held in my hand.
With the pollen of evening for a trail thence. Held in my hand.
At the *yuni*, the haliotis shell hangs with pollen. Held in my
    hand . . .[145]

The curious reader may discover among the notes that "kethawns are small sticks or cigarettes used by the Navahos as sacrifices to the gods," and that "yuni is the place of honor reserved for guests and the head of the house behind the fire opposite the door"; but the significance of the haliotis shell and the pollen cannot be fully comprehended unless one has a background of general Indian religious beliefs. Even the most capable ethnologist could hardly listen to this poetry with the same receptivity as could the native Navaho, and the connotations aroused by these words would be entirely different for white man and Indian. In the emotional sense, then, the feelings awakened by translated poetry cannot be carried over to another language and another race. From the above lines we may find aroused an intellectual curiosity about the vague-sounding words, and may possibly hazard our own interpretations of what the lines might mean; but to expect that we would properly grasp the emotional clues would be to expect that the Navaho would be touched exactly as we are by hearing in his own language a passage from the Twenty-third Psalm, or such a song as "My Love Is Like a Red, Red Rose."

Many allusions which are clear to the Indian are lost on the white man who lacks familiarity with such things as recreational background. Frederick Burton, one of the early students of Indian music, reported that he was baffled by a song whose only words were, "I use bad shoes." He concluded that this was a reference to worn-out footgear, and that the song was a plaint of poverty. Later he learned that it was the triumphant song of a skillful player of the moccasin game, and the idea was: "I am using bewitched shoes in the play: they will fool you; you're not smart enough to get around these wicked shoes of mine!" [33]

The story element in some ritual songs is not obvious unless the reader is familiar with the appropriate myths of the tribe. An example of this difficulty is found in the following Navaho "song of sequence":

SONG OF SEQUENCE [141]

Young Woman Who Becomes a Bear set fire in the mountains
In many places: as she journeyed on
There was a line of burning mountains.

The Otter set fire in the waters
In many places: as he journeyed on
There was a line of burning waters.

The explanation of meaning is given by the translator as follows:
"It is related that in the ancient days, during a year of great drought,
these holy ones, on their way to a council of the gods, set fire to the
mountains and the waters. The smoke arose in great clouds, from
which rain descended on the parched land." [141] Other examples of
mythological elements will be found in the various rituals given in
following chapters.

The meaning of an original Indian poem, then, is difficult to con-
vey into English not only because of the reader's unfamiliarity with
the everyday facts of Indian life, but also because Indian verse fre-
quently is intentionally cryptic, ambiguous, or esoteric. Insofar as
understanding the meanings of Indian poetry is a part of the total
value of the translations, in that proportion will the value of the
English version be marred by the sometimes unavoidable necessity
for the translator to omit certain allusions or to translate them
literally. To say that we cannot enjoy these poems in exactly the
same frame of mind as that in which they were composed by the
Indian, however, does not damage their poetic value in English or
their capacity for arousing esthetic satisfaction in the modern reader.

STYLE

Stylistic qualities may be found in Indian verse which parallel
those found in poetry in other languages. When the Aztec court
poet sang, "I colored with skill, I mingled choice roses in a noble
new song, polished like a jewel," he was thinking of poetic style as
a considered art.

Rhyme, in our sense of the word, is almost never found, but
other repetitional forms may be found to take its place and give, as
Spinden puts it, "an effect not of rhyming sounds but of rhyming
thoughts." [186] There is, as has been said, a rich use of metaphor and
other sense imagery. There is prominent in Indian verse an extreme
economy of expression which sometimes produces a poem that is little

more than a shorthand of ideas, implying nothing to the outsider but everything to the poet. Aside from repetition, stylistic devices such as contrast, monotony, variation, abbreviated expressions, poetic diction, parallelism, personification, apostrophe, euphony, and onomatopoeia are found which are used as they are used in European poetry. The best translations preserve a number of these effects, as may be seen in the selections in later chapters.

Many patterns may be discovered in Indian poetry, even in translation. Occasionally a pattern is achieved by a repeated refrain after every line; the most marked examples of this form are to be found in the Zuñi rituals in Chapter 4. Often, however, patterns of repetition with deft variation may be found, such as the Hopi "Discharming Song" in the same chapter. With this pattern, which resembles a child's block design, may be contrasted that of the Laguna "Corn Grinding Song," which has a clear but complex formula of repetition and variation. A more simple pattern emerges from the following Teton Sioux song:

I SING FOR THE ANIMALS [80]

> Out of the earth
> I sing for them,
> A Horse nation
> I sing for them.
> Out of the earth
> I sing for them,
> The animals
> I sing for them.

An odd poem from the stylistic point of view is "The Kayak Man's Abandoned Wife," which is discussed in Chapter 2.

Numerous devices of style are used by the Indians in their poems, and particular devices have come to be almost the conventional marks of certain tribes. Often the precise stylistic flavor is unavoidably lost in translation, and except for plain patterns, the literal translation of many tricks of Indian verse is frequently impossible. This is, of course, a truism to translators from languages other than Indian. The spirit of a piece of foreign literature is easier to reproduce than the precise style.

RHYTHM

Rhythm, though not of a finicky metrical sort, can be found by the expert in most Indian poetry. Although Indian verse is not composed in iambics or dactyls, the extensive researches of Frances Densmore,[56] who has published many volumes in musical notation, show that there is a measured rhythmic scheme for each type of Indian song. In the works of other qualified students there are remarks concerning the use of vocables added to "fill out the measures" in songs, and statements that accents could be misplaced in order to conform to the melodic scheme. It is hard to convince anyone who has listened hour after hour to the rising and falling chants and wails of an Indian ceremonial that such poetry lacks rhythm of a very marked, and perhaps very complicated, kind, a kind which is closely associated with the drum-beat.

Attempts to make exact metrical translations from Indian originals are seldom undertaken and are never completely satisfactory. In order to attain metrical equivalence, the translator must sacrifice considerable flexibility in treating the meaning and the style, and only at the expense of these important elements attains an approximation to the rhythm of the original.

The only translations appearing in this book which pretend to be rhythmic are those taken from the Hako ceremony of the Pawnee tribe. In these translations Miss Fletcher sought not only to make an English rendering in the rhythm of the original, but also to offer an interpretative version which supplies the connotations that might be aroused in the mind of the Indian initiate listening to the ceremonial and watching the placement of the various regalia. "A rhythmic rendition, which aims not only to convey the literal meaning but to embody the elucidations of the Kúrahus [leader of the ceremony] as well, has been made. Its words have been so chosen that the lines shall conform to the rhythm of the corresponding phrases of the song. This rendition is for the purpose of presenting to the eye and ear of the English reader the song as it appeals to the Pawnee who has been instructed in the rite." [90] Miss Fletcher's rhythmic rendition of the first stanza of one song is as follows:

> I know not if the voice of man can reach to the sky;
> I know not if the mighty one will hear as I pray;
> I know not if the gifts I ask will all granted be;
> I know not if the word of old we truly can hear;
> I know not what will come to pass in our future days;
> I hope that only good will come, my children, to you.

The Indian original of this stanza is given as:

> *Ho-o-o!*
> *Kakati chiri wakari pirau Tiráa;*
> *Kakati chiri wakari pirau Tiráa;*
> *Kakati chiri wakari pirau Tiráa;*
> *Kakati chiri wakari pirau Tiráa;*
> *Kakati chiri wakari pirau Tiráa;*
> *Kakati chiri wakari pirau Tiráa.*

It is evident that, whatever may be the closeness of rhythmic fidelity, the practice of supplying meanings which are merely implicit in the original is of doubtful validity. The variation and complicated thought of the translation is certainly not to be discovered in the literal one-sentence Indian stanza.

In this particular poem the translator has tried, perhaps, to retain too many attributes of Indian style; but she demonstrates that it is possible to render a metrical translation of this type of poetry. That this achievement has not been attained more often is probably a result of the fact that to most translators the successful interpretation of meaning and style takes precedence over merely metrical interest.

Sometimes it is possible for a translator to attain somewhat the same effect of the original meter by choosing a European meter which might be expected to arouse the same emotional attitude on the part of the listener. Ruth Bunzel remarks, concerning the rhythm of the Zuñi ritual prayers (see Chapter 4): "It has been impossible, of course, to render the original rhythm. One characteristic feature, however, has been retained, namely, its irregularity, the unsymmetrical alternation of long and short lines. . . . If one were to choose a familiar English verse form it should be the line

of Milton, or better still, the free verse of the King James version
of the Psalms. I have tried to retain the sense of the original of
the fluidity and variety of the verse form." [32] This translator also
speaks of the lengthy sentences possible in the highly inflected
Zuñi language, and states that "the reader should think of the
Zuñi sentence rolling on like the periods of a Ciceronian oration
to their final close." [32]

Indian poetry, then, has rhythm which approaches meter, but
it is seldom that a translator tries to reproduce the exact rhythm
of the original. It is more profitable to try to give the effect of the
original by selecting, from traditional English line forms, a rhythm
that will suggest the tone of the native verse.

SUCCESS OF BEST TRANSLATORS

How successful are the best translations of Indian poetry?

The reader can answer this question for himself when he has
read the selections in later chapters. To appreciate this poetry as
poetry, it is not necessary that one have a knowledge of the Indian
languages from which it was taken; it is requisite only to judge the
translated verses as contributions to American literature. We do
the same thing when we speak of the style or poetic qualities of
the King James version of the Bible, which all of us can appreciate
without having to know the Hebrew or Greek originals from which
it was made.

If the Indian poems are compared with other translations into
English from primitive or early verse, such as the Anglo-Saxon
elegies or the ancient Greek religious poems, a fair basis for judg-
ment can be attained. Obviously it would be of little worth to
compare a Matthews version of a Navaho ritual with any of the
best English translations of Dante's *Divine Comedy*. If, however,
the primitive Indian religious verses in translation are set side by
side with equally competent translations of pagan Greek hymns
of the time of Hesiod, it is likely that the Navahos will not suffer
by the comparison.

The success of the translations offered herein may be judged from several points of view, such as the literal closeness of the translation to the original; the skill with which such features of the original as meaning, verbal style, or metrical effect are carried over into English; the value of the translation in comparison with translations from other primitive verse; and the worth of these translations of Indian poetry as contributions to the main body of American literature. It is from this last point of view that the selections which are later given will be discussed, although the other three points of view will not be neglected when occasion is offered to mention particular effects. In short, the selections will be considered primarily as American poetry from a native and non-European tradition, poetry which has grown from the needs and ideals of American Indian religious and social life.

THE STUDY OF INDIAN POETRY

During the past hundred years an impressive body of first-rate translations from Indian poetry has grown up; almost all of the best translations have been made by professional ethnologists who have united with their linguistic knowledge a talent for literary rendition of the native originals.

Although Prescott published as early as 1843 an English version of an Aztec poem in the appendix to his *Conquest of Mexico*, the beginning of wide interest in native poetry in translation properly dates from the year 1851, when a history of the Indians was published by Henry Rowe Schoolcraft which included samples of Chippewa poetry. Schoolcraft had married the granddaughter of a chief of this tribe, and from her he had learned many of the native legends and songs. In his *Algic Researches* (1839) he had already published an essay on "The Myth of Hiawatha" which undoubtedly inspired Longfellow's popular *Song of Hiawatha* (1855), America's best known poem on an Indian subject. (It should be emphasized that the meter chosen by Longfellow was adapted from the Finnish epic *Kalevala*, and bore no resemblance to the verse form of any American Indian tribal poetry.)

The genesis of a part of *Hiawatha* which will be recalled by many a reader of Longfellow is found in Schoolcraft's monumental work of 1851. The scheme of Schoolcraft's presentation of this little song follows a pattern still used by students of Indian verse—original text, literal translation, and literary translation, as follows:

CHANT TO THE FIRE-FLY [175]
(*Chippewa original*)

> *Wau wau tay see!*
> *Wau wau tay see!*
> *E mow e shin*
> *Tahe bwau ne baun-e wee!*
> *Be eghaun—be eghaun—ewee!*
> *Wau wau tay see!*
> *Wau wau tay see!*
> *Was sa koon ain je gun.*
> *Was sa koon ain je gun.*

(*Literal translation*)

Flitting-white-fire-insect! waving-white-fire-bug! give me light before I go to bed! give me light before I go to sleep. Come, little dancing white-fire-bug! Come, little flitting white-fire-beast! Light me with your bright white-flame-instrument —your little candle.

(*Literary translation*)

Fire-fly, fire-fly! bright little thing,
Light me to bed, and my song I will sing.
Give me your light, as you fly o'er my head,
That I may merrily go to my bed.
Give me your light o'er the grass as you creep,
That I may joyfully go to my sleep.
Come, little fire-fly, come, little beast—
Come! and I'll make you tomorrow a feast.
Come, little candle that flies as I sing,
Bright little fairy-bug—night's little king;
Come, and I'll dance as you guide me along,
Come, and I'll pay you, my bug, with a song.

Schoolcraft's friend Charles Fenno Hoffman also took a hand in translating several Chippewa poems from this material; he is assumed to be the author of an often published piece, "Calling-One's-Own."

Thirty years passed before the branch of study initiated by Schoolcraft was the subject of further serious research; and interest in the words of Indian songs then sprang from a previous interest in Indian melody. Oddly, the first analytical study of American Indian music was made by a German and was published in Germany. This man was Theodor Baker, who came to the United States in 1880, spent the summer among the Seneca Indians of New York, and later visited the Indian School at Carlisle, Pennsylvania. The result of his inquiries was published in 1882 under the title of *Ueber die Musik der Nordamerikanischen Wilden*. It was not chiefly concerned with the texts of songs, but with the music.

In 1883, Daniel G. Brinton, in his paper *Aboriginal American Authors*, called attention to the fact that the American continents had a native literature, and in brief space supported his declaration that "the languages of America and the literary productions in those languages have every whit as high a claim on the attention of European scholars as have the venerable documents of Chinese lore, the mysterious cylinders of Assyria, or the painted and figured papyri of the Nilotic tombs." In the same year he began the publication of the "Library of American Aboriginal Literature," which under his editorship reached eight volumes by 1890; several of these volumes, such as Horatio Hale's *Iroquois Book of Rites* and Brinton's own translations from Lenape and Aztec literature, are devoted to poetry or contain poetic passages.

In 1884, Miss Alice Cunningham Fletcher began her distinguished career as a collector, arranger, and translator of Indian songs with the publication of a paper on "The 'Wawan' or Pipe Dances of the Omahas," which offered a study of ten Indian melodies. This resulted from a visit among the Omahas the previous year, during which she obtained the co-operation of a son of the head chief; this young member of the tribe, Francis La Flesche, whose grandfather had been a French trader, thus began a career as an ethnologist in his own right which enabled him to become the foremost person of Indian blood to labor in the preservation and translation of native poetry. His collaboration with Miss Fletcher continued until her death in 1922. She became widely known for such works as "A Study of Omaha Indian Music" (1893) and "The Hako: A Pawnee Ceremony" (1904). Her interest in translating texts, however, was subordinate to her interest in musical forms.

In 1887, John Reade in two papers included in the *Transactions* of the Royal Society of Canada offered some general observations on the study of Indian poetry, and presented two Wabanaki poems which he had collected. In the same year, Dr. Washington Matthews, one of the greatest of the early translators of Indian poetry, published his paper on "The Mountain Chant: A Navaho Ceremony" in the *Annual Report* of the Bureau of Ethnology of the Smithsonian Institution. Dr. Matthews was one of those rare authors that combine a knowledge of Indian linguistics with high talent in translating native verse with power and taste, and his success did much to stimulate other collectors to try their skill. The best of his later work is in *The Night Chant* (1902), an analysis of another Navaho ceremonial, and in "Navaho Myths, Prayers, and Songs" (1907).

In 1888, several important investigations were published or initiated. J. Owen Dorsey issued a paper on Ponka and Omaha songs, the first of a series of studies. Franz Boas, one of the soundest students of primitive poetry, published a paper on Chinook songs, as well as a work on the Central Eskimo which included a discussion of their verses. He also, in a series of papers a few years later, called attention to the translations into English of Eskimo songs which had been published as early as 1875 by Dr. Heinrich Rink, a Danish scientist. In 1888, Carlos Troyer went to live among the Zuñi Indians, where he collected songs which, published in 1913 with piano accompaniment, introduced Indian songs to the concert platform.

Another important year for publication was 1891, when Walter Hoffman presented his study of the Midéwiwin medicine society of the Chippewas. Benjamin Ives Gilman gave a paper on Zuñi songs which was, however, mainly concerned with the melodies rather than the words. In this same year James Mooney published his remarkable monograph, "Sacred Formulas of the Cherokees," which contained a number of curious charms and curative incantations translated from the written language of this tribe (these studies were continued in his paper on "The Swimmer Manuscript," 1932). Mooney is also known as the most important collector of the vision-inspired songs of the Ghost Dance Religion (1896).

In 1893, the best known collector of North American Indian songs, Frances Densmore, began her work, inspired by reading Alice Fletcher's studies. Miss Densmore, who had been a piano teacher and church organist, encouraged by Miss Fletcher and prepared by a course of reading, began to visit among the Chippewa and Sioux tribes during vacation periods, and recorded in conventional notation the songs she heard. In 1907 she began a series of researches under the Smithsonian Institution which has continued to the present time and has taken her to many tribes. Among her long list of publications may be noted her monographs on the music of the Chippewa, Papago, Pawnee, and Sioux tribes. Although Miss Densmore is predominantly interested in the melodic and harmonic aspects of her subject, she is a skilled translator and her observations on the general subject of Indian poetry are highly authoritative.

Passing attention was given to Indian verse during the next few years, the most interesting translations being those of Charles Godfrey Leland and John Dyneley Prince in *Kuloskap the Master and Other Algonkin Poems* (1902). Some of these verses are metrical; the better ones are not. Original texts are usually given, but the general remarks of the translators are now outmoded.

The Indians' Book by Natalie Curtis (Burlin) first appeared in 1907, containing translations and music of songs from a number of tribes. The following year, Frank Russell's literary translations of Pima songs were published. In 1909, *American Primitive Music*, by Frederick R. Burton, appeared, a volume less concerned with texts than with musical characteristics.

With the exception of various good textual studies by Edward Sapir, Frank G. Speck, John R. Swanton, and Pliny Earle Goddard, there was a lapse until the year 1918, when popular attention to the subject was widely aroused by the appearance of the first anthology of Indian verse, *The Path on the Rainbow*, edited by George Cronyn.

This volume was highly uncritical. The editor appeared to think that the Ojibway and Chippewa were two different tribes; he included as an "Eskimo ballad" a literal translation of a folk tale; and first among his selections from the American Southwest was an ancient *Inca* song from Peru. Moreover, the writer of the Introduction quoted as indubitably American the notorious "Marriage Song of Tikaens," exposed as a forgery as early as 1890.

Although this first anthology was not well edited, and although it lumped with the sound translations of scholars a number of "interpretations" by contemporary American poets which had slight value either as interpretations or as first-rate modern verse, the presentation of these samples of Indian poetry stirred comment in the literary journals. Interest was heightened by the fact that several of the poems in the anthology happened to fit the canons of a literary movement known as Imagism which had been started several years before, whose proponents found in short verses like the Chippewa songs collected by Miss Densmore the sort of compressed word-pictures they also sought in other foreign forms like the Chinese poems collected by Ernest Fenellosa and the rigid seventeen-syllable Japanese form called the *haiku*. Although the presentation of an image in a few terse lines is clearly not the invention of the Imagist or any other school of poetry, resemblances can be found between the most highly admired Imagist poems and certain "primitive" forms from America and Asia. The most obvious common trait arises from the idea that a poem should contain no irrelevant words. Carried to an extreme, this leads to the use of a sort of lyric shorthand that may make the poem incomprehensible or, sometimes, merely odd. The danger of excessive abbreviation is that, unless the reader is able to share the experience of the poet, the symbol requires a lengthy gloss, and the need for a lengthy explanation of the meaning destroys the lightning-like impact of the verse. Some Imagist poems of two lines had to be "explained" by their authors in twenty lines of prose. The problem of making poems which allude to commonplaces of Indian thought meaningful to the white reader has already been mentioned, to show why it will be often necessary to explain at length the particular background of idea and circumstance from which an Indian poem has sprung.

An examination of contemporary "interpretations" of Indian verse-forms seems to show that attempts by white poets, who have not lived among the Indians and studied their beliefs and styles of expression, to imitate Indian poetry are foredoomed to failure. A white poet living today simply cannot put himself inside the skin and brain of the Indian and sing as he would sing. The value of studying the rich store of authentic translations of Indian song might, however, be great. The use of intense and implicative phrases by poets such as Yvor Winters, Sarah Unna, and Hart Crane, who were not avowed Imagists or "interpreters" but who were familiar with the best translations of Indian verse, shows what might be done to use this really "American" source of poetic inspiration. A poet today could learn much if he entered into rivalry with the best Indian poets in such qualities as compactness of expression, keenness of observation, use of apt metaphor, serious handling of serious subjects, and reverence before the revealed beauties of nature.

The publication of *The Path on the Rainbow* did arouse considerable popular interest in the translating of Indian poetry which had been carried on by professional ethnologists and linguists since Schoolcraft's day. As a result, it not only turned the attention of poets to the potentialities of Indian subjects and rhythms, but stimulated the scientific students of Indian life to prepare literary translations of the verses they collected.

In 1921 Francis La Flesche, who had collaborated with Alice Fletcher ten years before in writing the monograph "The Omaha Tribe," began the publication of four voluminous studies of the rites of the Osage tribe, and these were followed in 1939 with his excellent volume on *War Ceremony and Peace Ceremony of the Osage Indians*. In 1921, also, Nellie Barnes published the results of a doctoral investigation on "American Indian Verse: Characteristics of Style," which was followed in 1925 by an anthology of this verse, *American Indian Love Lyrics.* In 1923, Mrs. Mary Austin had published a small volume, *The American Rhythm,* an impressionistic and rhapsodic attempt to work out an esthetic for the Indian rhythmic arts.

A notable contribution to the translation into English of the Eskimo songs of South Greenland was made in 1923 with the publication of *The Ammassalik Eskimo,* by William Thalbitzer. This author, a Dane, made excellent studies in the field pioneered by his countryman Dr. Rink, and his various volumes contain the best survey of Eskimo poetry to be found in English.

Since 1923 a number of important volumes and monographs have been published by professional ethnologists which add to the store of translations of Indian poetry. Most of these, naturally, give only literal translations, word for word, without an attempt to realize the literary possibilities of the material. It is seldom that scientific accuracy and literary taste are combined so harmoniously as to produce such translations as those of Herbert J. Spinden, whose *Songs of the Tewa* came out in 1933. Among the many scholars who have given literal versions of texts are Ruth L. Bunzel, John Hubert Cornyn, Berard Haile, George Herzog, Harry Hoijer, Clyde Kluckhohn, Alice Marriott, and Ruth M. Underhill.

The seeker for translations of Indian songs must hunt in many places. The bibliography given in this volume, which contains more than two hundred items on North American Indian verse, for the first time collects these references and shows the amount of study which has been given to American Indian poetry in translation.

2

ESKIMOS OF THE ARCTIC COASTS

POETRY AND MUSIC play an important part in the lives of the
Eskimos, the native race that dwells on the coasts and islands of
Arctic America from East Greenland to the westernmost Aleutian
Islands.

The Eskimos, who live cheerful and peaceful lives on these barren
and ice-locked shores, are a type markedly different from other
American aborigines. It was long thought that they had migrated
from Asia in a rather recent epoch, but from what we now know,
it seems that their culture centered in Greenland and spread west-
ward. They are unique in being the only American group that are
surely known to have had contact with white people before the
coming of Columbus, for Greenland was occupied as early as the
tenth century by Norsemen.

Although the Eskimos have some permanent settlements, in
summer they must travel in search of the caribou and musk ox, living
in skin tents spread on poles, and in winter they take shelter in the
famed igloos or in earth-roofed excavations, making forays in fair
weather against the seal and often camping on the frozen sea. The
men hunt and fish; all other household duties are carried on by the
women.

Their rugged lives have sharpened their powers of invention; almost universally known among the Eskimos are the kayak and the large "woman's boat," the oil lamp, the harpoon, the drill, the fishing float, sewn skin garments, and the dog sled. They are artists with tools; they cleverly carve masks, boxes, and bowls, and make fine drawings and carved pictures. And, paddling on the bitter sea or snug in winter lodgings, they joyfully make poetry.

The songs and recitations of the Eskimos are especially rich in the observation of nature for nature's sake, a mainspring of poetry seldom found among their native neighbors to the southward. They have also composed hunting songs and magical incantations, work songs, children's songs, and game songs. Their sense of humor and mimicry is well developed, and often they carry on long comic pantomimes. Satire is highly sharpened in them, and their "drum-songs" are a strange sort of trial by poetry, a bloodless duel in verse. Eskimo poetry has been translated by Heinrich Rink, Franz Boas, and William Thalbitzer.

More than a touch of noble contemplation of natural beauty is found in two songs from Greenland:

MOUNT KOONAK: A SONG OF ARSUT [167]

I look toward the south, to great Mount Koonak,
To great Mount Koonak, there to the south;
I watch the clouds that gather round him;
I contemplate their shining brightness;
They spread abroad upon great Koonak;
They climb up his seaward flanks;
See how they shift and change;
Watch them there to the south;
How one makes beautiful the other;
How they mount his southern slopes,
Hiding him from the stormy sea,
Each lending beauty to the other.

A SONG FROM SANERUT [167]

I behold yon land of Nunarsuit.
The mountain tops on its south side are wrapped in clouds.
It slopes toward the south,

Toward Usuarsuk.
What couldst thou expect in such a miserable place?
All its surroundings being shrouded with ice,
Not before late in the spring can people from there go traveling.

Another nature poem, "Song from Southern Sermilik," which seems to show European influence, has been given in Chapter 1.

A compressed sketch from nature which might well compare with those of the Imagist school of American poets of yesteryear is this picture of a Greenland bird:

THE WHEAT-EAR [197]

The naughty wheat-ear
From its nest
Comes quickly out.
Wiutiu! it whistles.

Here is an Eskimo impression of the sight of a shooting-star:

THE SHOOTING-STAR [195]

You star up yonder,
You who gaze up yonder,
Your fingers up yonder,
Didn't hold very fast,
Didn't knit very tight.
It fell down without touching,
Without entirely touching against—
It didn't touch.

Another song with a strong lyrical content was, in fact, a chant of thanksgiving; it was made by a young man who when sealing went adrift on the ice, and did not reach shore until after a week of hardship.

I AM JOYFUL [18]

Aja, I am joyful; this is good!
Aja, there is nothing but ice around me, that is good!
Aja, I am joyful; this is good!
My country is nothing but slush, that is good!
Aja, I am joyful; this is good!

Aja, when, indeed, will this end? This is good!
I am tired of watching and waking, this is good!

A woman of South Greenland, while picking berries on the fells,
is stricken by a sad memory. High above the settlement she looks
down the coast, watches the kayaks floating on the quiet sea, and
voices her melancholy.

SONG AT THE BERRY-PICKING ON THE MOUNTAIN [195]

Great grief came over me—
Great grief came over me,
While on the fell above us I was picking berries.
Great grief came over me.
My sun quickly rose over it.
Great sorrow came over me.
The sea out there off our settlement
Was beautifully quiet—
And the great, dear paddlers
Were leaving out there—
Great grief came over me
While I was picking berries on the fell.

The style of native American poetry is not always crude; indeed,
it is often subtle. By repetition of certain words, the following poem
gives the effect of advancing and retreating voices. Two persons
are carrying on a loud dialog; one speaker, a woman, stands on a
rock on shore and shouts to a man who chances to paddle past in
his kayak. The translator explains that some words are repeated
three or four times to show the difficulty of the two speakers in
understanding each other's words at a distance. Other readers may
rather get the effect of words reverberating along shore from head-
land to headland; why should not this be truly an echo song?

THE KAYAK MAN'S ABANDONED WIFE [195]

Listen you down there, listen you down there!
Listen, you kayak, kayak, kayak!
Where, where, where is your wife?—
I have left her, have left her, have left her.—
Whither, whither, whither?—

In the woman's boat, in the woman's boat!—
Why, why, why?—
Because she nearly was dead from cold, nearly was dead from cold,
And she ever and always was with child.
She was clad in a jacket of a young crested seal.
Let the presented piece of blubber only drive farther away with
    the stream!—
Far away to the distance!

The next to the last line may be confusing. It refers to the present of
a piece of blubber which one hunter's wife gives to another in
friendship, to provide extra food for an emergency.

    The Eskimo religion is primitive. They believe that a powerful
old woman lives in the sea, who can punish offenders against her
taboos by bringing storms, or by hiding from the hunters the sea
animals over which she rules as a goddess. The chief duty of the
angekoks or magic-working priests is to smell out the infringers of
taboos and make them confess. The Eskimo believes that two spirits
reside in the body, one which stays with it when it dies and may
temporarily enter the body of some child who is then given the
name of the departed, and another which may go to the land of
souls. Sickness is caused by the loss of the soul, which may explain
the following healing chant:

AGAINST SICKNESS [195]

    What approaches me?
    The hound of the dawn approaches me.
    Put my dog's harness on it,
    Send off Asiartik!
    You are sent off, and well on the way.
    What approaches me?
    The star's hound approaches me.
    Put my dog's harness on it,
    Send off Asiartik!
    You are sent off and well on the way.

The meaning seems to be this: "The hound of the dawn approaches;
put my dog's harness on it, and drive in a sledge out to the horizon
to fetch home the sick person's lost soul!"

Here is a magic formula used by a woman the first time she began to sew again after a period of mourning. The idea is familiar as compulsive magic; the primitive mind believes that if you say you have special powers, these powers will be granted to you.

A WOMAN'S FIRST SEWING AFTER A MOURNING [195]

Whose claws have I for pinch-fingers?
The bat's claws I have for pinch-fingers,
On account of my housewife work.
Whose claws have I for pinch-fingers?
The crab's claws I have for pinch-fingers,
On account of my housewife work.

Incantations to insure good hunting, as will be shown, were common among all natives from the Arctic to the Equator. An example is this charm which the hunter hoped would subdue the fierceness of the walrus, so that it might be easily harpooned when the close fighting began:

WALRUS HUNTING [195]

The walrus, I harpoon it,
Stroking its cheek.
You have become quiet and meek.
The walrus, I harpoon it,
Patting its tusks.
You have become quiet and meek.

The native who reported this song was cynical about its value. "I tried to make the charm work," he remarked, "but I never succeeded in killing a walrus!"

Among the translations of native songs from America are few secular songs which were sung to accompany a rhythmic task, like the chanteys which our seamen of the old sailing days trolled while pushing round the capstan, or the choruses sung by stevedores as they rolled the cotton bales. Perhaps these songs did exist among the Indians but were too trivial to be preserved or collected. It is more likely that such songs were almost always ritual or religious in nature, and were designed to be chanted, like the corn-grinding songs in Chapter 4, in a ceremonial form that would bring success to the work. At any rate, in spite of our romantic ideas about canoe-paddling songs and the like, the only work songs discovered from North America are these two from the Eskimos:

THE KAYAK PADDLER'S JOY AT THE WEATHER [195]

>When I'm out of the house in the open,
>>I feel joy.
>When I get out on the sea on haphazard,
>>I feel joy.
>If it is really fine weather,
>>I feel joy.
>If the sky really clears nicely,
>>I feel joy.
>May it continue thus
>>for the good of my sealing!
>May it continue thus
>>for the good of my hunting!
>May it continue thus
>>for the good of my singing-match!
>May it continue thus
>>for the good of my drum-song!

The reference to the "drum-song" will be made clear in a later paragraph. The poem may be contrasted with the following bad-weather song, in which the singer says that his victorious chant was already clear in his mind, but he was unable to use it because foul weather spoiled all chance of a lucky hunt.

THE PADDLER'S SONG ON BAD HUNTING WEATHER [195]

>I got my poem in perfect order.
>On the threshold of my tongue
>Its arrangement was made.
>But I failed, indeed, in my hunting.
>The brewing storm-clouds in the ocean sky,
>The north sky's gathering sleet clouds—
>I noticed the heavy mists which gathered hurriedly;
>When they arise,
>When they roll across the mountain-sides,
>They are the north sky's gathering sleet clouds.

A number of noteworthy little songs to sing to children are found among the Eskimos. A distinct type of nursery poem is called the "petting-song." The following modern petting-song for a boy child was composed by a recently widowed woman who had no son. She could expect to suffer real want without a boy to support her as he grew up. If, according to native belief, a son were born to her brother, shortly after the death of her husband, the child would be named after the lately departed one, and as his namesake would become the foster-child of the widow. This happened; and from joy over this lucky chance, she made the song to honor the baby, her future provider.

PETTING-SONG (MODERN) [195]

How charming he is, that little pet there!
How charming he is—
How amazing he is, the dear little creature!

How bland he is and gentle, the great little one there!
How bland he is and gentle—
How amazing he is, the dear little creature!

How sound he looks and vigorous, the great little thing there!
How sound he looks and vigorous!
How amazing he is, the dear little creature!

A children's game song to accompany finger play is also given:

FINGER GAME [197]

You thumb there, wake up!
The kayak-rowers are about to leave you!
Forefinger there, wake up!
The umiak-rowers are about to leave you!
Middle finger there, wake up!
The wood-gatherers are about to leave you!
Ring-finger there, wake up!
The berry-gatherers are about to leave you!
Little finger there, wake up!
The crake-heather-gatherers are about to leave you!

The "nith-song" or "drum-song" is the Eskimo's way of replacing a law court by a public poetry contest. One imagines that there would be fewer suits at law in our own world if each party were required to state his grievances in satirical verse before an audience that would arbitrate the issue on the basis of the disputant's power of poetically arousing sympathy for himself and ridicule for his opponent.

The background of the nith-song (from the Norwegian *nith*, meaning "contention"), observed as early as 1746, has been described as follows: "When a Greenlander considers himself injured in any way by another person, he composes about him a satirical song, which he rehearses with the help of his intimates. He then challenges the offending one to a duel of song. One after another the two disputants sing at each other their wisdom, wit, and satire, supported by their partisans, until at last one is at his wit's end, when the audience, who are the jury, make known their decision. The matter is now settled for good, and the contestants must be friends again and not recall the matter which was in dispute. . . . The fear of public shame is very powerful as a factor in social betterment. This remarkable restriction of vengeance and modification of the duel has been largely overlooked by sociologists." [121]

Since among the Eskimos there was no tribal police force for carrying out the laws, and individual revenge was expected, this bloodless way of settling feuds did have great social value. This form of verbal tournament, which might well have been mentioned by William James in his essay on "A Moral Equivalent for War," was often so successful that the loser, publicly shamed by his sharp-tongued opponent, left the neighborhood to avoid remaining a laughingstock. As a literary form it may be compared to the "flytings" found in northern literatures, such as the response of Beowulf to Unferth, and to the scurrilous Scottish "Flyting of Dunbar and Kennedie," an extreme form of the popular medieval tenzon which displayed the satiric skill of rival troubadours.

Two writers in English, Rink and Thalbitzer, both Danes, have collected and made the best translations of these "drum-songs," so called because the singer accompanied himself on a drum. Perhaps the best known of these is a revision by Thalbitzer of an earlier version by Rink. The first speaker ridicules the accent of his oppo-

nent, who retaliates by charges of cowardice and ingratitude after a
rescue at sea.

NITH-SONG OF SAVDLAT AND PULANGIT-SISSOK [22, 167]

(Savdlat speaks)

The south shore, O yes, the south shore I know it;
Once I lived there and met Pulangit-Sissok,
A fat fellow who lived on halibut, O yes, I know him.
Those south-shore folks can't talk;
They don't know how to pronounce our language;
Truly they are dull fellows;
They don't even talk alike;
Some have one accent, some another;
Nobody can understand them;
They can scarcely understand each other.

(Pulangit-Sissok speaks)

O yes, Savdlat and I are old acquaintances;
He wishes me extremely well at times;
Once I know he wished I was the best boatman on the shore;
It was a rough day and I in mercy took his boat in tow;
Ha! ha! Savdlat, thou didst cry most pitiful;
Thou wast awfully afeared;
In truth, thou wast nearly upset;
And hadst to keep hold of my boat strings,
And give me part of thy load.
O yes, Savdlat and I are old acquaintances.

A number of drum-songs, whose humorous points are sometimes
difficult to get because they are literally translated, are given by
Thalbitzer. Of these the following have been chosen:

DRUM-SONG ABOUT A STUPID KAYAK PADDLER [195]

I always envy them when I hear them sing their drum-songs.
I amount to nothing.
Surely yes,—the art of making poems,
The art of "capsizing,"
For that I am not fitted.

The intended irony here may be stated in prose something like this: "I may not be proficient in singing, but neither am I notorious in the clumsy handling of my kayak."

Another satirical poem casts reflections upon the skill of the opponent in the art of hunting.

THE REAL SLAYER OF THE SEAL [195]

How is it with him, your Alapa?
I heard him shout for help,
When he had bound your catch, the hooded seal,
Shouting aloud
That he had bound a hooded seal to a little iceberg,
That he had slain it.
Your catch down there,
It was I who plunged my lance into it.
It flopped terribly.

The following mocking drum-song is apparently a dialog, of satirical challenge and shamefaced response.

COMPLAINT OVER BAD HUNTING [195]

How is it with you?
Are you, I wonder, a man? Are you, I wonder, a real male?—
My throw [with the weapon] is not smooth and firm,
I cannot get hold of the seals.—
How is it with you?
Are you, I wonder, a man? Are you a real male?—
These whales and walruses I cannot get hold of.

The next drum-song seems to have been composed in revenge for an act of violence.

MUTUAL CHARGES OF MOLESTATION [195]

Gossip spreads my name, it is said,
I am said to be a manslayer.
Gossip spreads my name, it is said,
I am said to be a murderer.
This they say of me; it is nothing new:
I have no discretion, no circumspection.

Since I had no big words about it,
They say I have said: All right! Try it!
Make a little trial with me, please!
If only you do not wound anyone, please,
If only I am not so unfortunate as to be wounded.
Your feather-harpoon is wont to strike hard.
Why this pain within me?

The irony of the phrase concerning the harpoon which strikes with
the impact of a feather is unmistakable. It is probable that this song
was accompanied by action and gesture, and that the singer acted out
the pain of being stricken, thus adding to the audience's pleasure the
element of clownish pantomime.

The following piece is a humorous dialog between a wheat-ear and
a snow-bird, and might be considered as an imaginary nith-song duel
between two feathered contestants. It may be compared to such
medieval tenzons as "The Owl and the Nightingale."

THE WHEAT-EAR AND THE SNOW-BIRD [197]

Whom can I get to husband,
Him with the lofty forehead,
Him with the many hairs [the shaggy one],
Him without trousers?

Me,
Will you have me to husband?
I who myself have a lofty forehead,
I who myself have many hairs,
I who myself am without trousers?

You,
I do not want you to husband
Because you have so lofty a forehead,
Because you have so many hairs,
Because you are completely without trousers!

Just as she said that,
At the same moment as she related that,—
Quak! Quak!

This sampling of the drum-songs of the Eskimo may be concluded with the diverting flyting-song of Kuk-Ook, the bad boy, against the relatives who have punished him:

THE SONG OF KUK-OOK, THE BAD BOY [167]

This is the song of Kuk-Ook, the bad boy.
>*Imakayah—hayah,*
>*Imakayah—hah—hayah.*

I am going to run away from home, *hayah,*
In a great big boat, *hayah,*
To hunt for a sweet little girl, *hayah;*
I shall get her some beads, *hayah;*
The kind that look like boiled ones, *hayah;*
Then after a while, *hayah,*
I shall come back home, *hayah,*
I shall call all my relations together, *hayah,*
And shall give them all a good thrashing, *hayah;*
I shall marry two girls at once, *hayah;*
One of the sweet little darlings, *hayah,*
I shall dress in spotted seal-skins, *hayah,*
And the other dear little pet, *hayah,*
Shall wear skins of the hooded seal only, *hayah.*

3

TOTEM-POLE MAKERS OF THE NORTHWEST

GROTESQUELY carved totem poles mark the villages of the culture group extending southward on the Pacific Coast from southern Alaska to Oregon. Living out their lives on salt water or in the shadow of the rainy cedar forests, these hunters and fishers were until recent times left to themselves, untouched by white-man ways, and sang the same kinds of songs that were sung by their revered tribal ancestors.

The northernmost of these tribes—Tlingit, Haida, and Tsimshian —are the most typical in culture. The central group are the Kwakiutl. Further south, the Makah, Chinook, and a few other tribes were most influenced by white ways; indeed, the Chinook jargon was long used by traders on this coast as a kind of lingua franca. These coast tribes lived on seals, dried fish, clams, and berries, boiling their food by dropping hot stones into pits, boxes, or spruce-root baskets. The straight-grained, fragrant wood of the cedar challenged their sense of craftsmanship, and with crude tools of stone and bone they felled these great trees and shaped them to their needs. Not only were they carved into the totemic designs of bear, whale, beaver, and eagle found on their tall emblems of family pride, but the logs were split into planks from which high-gabled quadrangular houses were erected, in which a large family might live. Other carving was lavished upon masks and rattles. From large trunks of cedar, seagoing dugouts, some with sails, were hollowed. The bark of the cedar was used for clothing and robes; skin clothing was sometimes worn, although the beautiful robes of sea otter fur which brought the ships of seven nations to this coast in 1787 are now only a memory. Their weapons were bow, club, and dagger, and they made crude body armor and helmets.

Their social lives were dominated by the magic of shamans and the rites of secret societies. The most powerful cult was the Cannibal Society, in which the initiates were supposed to be driven by a gluttony that in the olden times was cannibalistic indeed. To these tribesmen, everything—family name, privileges, wives, slaves, and sheets of carved copper—had its price, and the higher the price, the greater the value in their eyes. Of all Indians, only this northwestern group have set up greed as a virtue.

The kinds of poems from the Pacific Northwest of special interest are curing charms, love songs, mourning songs, satirical songs (especially those in which the singer boasts of his wealth), and many fine songs for children. The best translators in this area are Franz Boas and John R. Swanton.

Songs were frequently used by shamans or magic healers in their treatment of a patient, as was universal among the native North Americans. Typical is this Kwakiutl curing ritual. The first two verses were sung as the shaman entered carrying a hemlock ring for purifying the patient and walked up to him; the third was sung while the ring was put over the patient; and the fourth while the shaman walked around the fire with the ring. Afterward the ring was thrown into the fire, while the watchers beat time.

SHAMAN'S SONG [19]

I have been told to continue to heal him, by the good supernatural
    power.
I have been told to keep on putting the hemlock ring over him, by
    the Shaman-of-the-Sea, the good supernatural power.

I have been told to put back into our friend his soul, by the good
supernatural power.
I have been told to give him long life, by the Long-Life-Giver-of-
the-Sea, the Chief-of-High-Water, the good supernatural power.

"Put our friend through the ring." Thus I was told by the super-
natural power.
"Spray our friend!" Thus I was told by the supernatural power.
"Heal our friend!" Thus I was told by the supernatural power.
"Take out [the weakness] of our friend!" Thus I was told by the
supernatural power.

I come and bring back this means of bringing to life our friend,
Supernatural Power.
Come now means-of-bringing-to-life of our Shaman-of-the-Sea of
our friend, Supernatural Power.
Make well all over our friend, that no ill may befall our poor friend,
Supernatural Power.
Now you will protect our poor friend, that he may walk safely,
Supernatural Power.

Now, Supernatural Power, cure our poor friend and make him well
again, O Great Real Supernatural Power, Supernatural Power.
Now, Supernatural Power, turn him the right way and make well our
friend here, you, Great Real Supernatural Power, Healer-of-
the-Sea.
Now take this, Supernatural Power, Spirit-of-the-Fire, this which
will cure our friend here, you, Great Real Supernatural Power,
Fire-Spirit-Woman.
And do protect our friend, you, Fire-Spirit-Woman, Great Super-
natural Power.

Glorification of romantic love, as will be explained in a later
chapter, was almost never found in Indian poetry. Consequently,
"Indian love calls" are fantasies of the white man or were recently
superimposed by him upon native ideas. Examples of modern in-
fluences on Chinook love songs were shown in Chapter 1. Similar
brief love plaints, which are strongly touched by modern life, are
here given from the Tlingits.

WHY HAVE I COME TO YOU? [194]

Why have I come to you to Dyea from far inland only to find
    that you have gone away to another town [on a steamer]?
Here I am, crying for you.

Another one was composed by Raven-Skin when his sweetheart
abandoned him:

WOLF WOMAN [194]

If one had control of death, it would be very easy to die with
    a Wolf woman.
It would be very pleasant.

Here is a "very modern" love song:

MY DEAR TOMMY [194]

I don't care about anything since even my dear boy, my dear
    Tommy, has gone from me.

The last one of this group was composed by Man-That-Is-Not-All-
Right, about Princess Thom, because "when she was very young all
sorts of young men went to her house, filling it as if it were a saloon."

RAVEN WOMAN [194]

Even from a saloon people get away, but not from you,
    Raven Woman.

A Kwakiutl love song of the coast made by a man who was
jilted, and the lady's retort to it, shows an odd use of refrain with
variations.

LOVE SONG [19]

Oh, how, my lady-love, can my thoughts be conveyed to you, my
    lady-love, on account of your deed, my lady-love?
In vain, my lady-love, did I wish to advise you, my lady-love, on
    account of your deed, my lady-love.
It is the object of laughter, my lady-love, it is the object of laughter,
    your deed, my lady-love.
It is the object of contempt, my lady-love, it is the object of
    contempt, your deed, my lady-love.
Oh, if poor me could go, my lady-love! How can I go to you, my
    lady-love, on account of your deed, my lady-love?

Oh, if poor me could go, my lady-love, to make you happy, my
lady-love, on account of your deed, my lady-love!

Now, I will go, my lady-love, go to make you happy, my lady-love,
on account of your deed, my lady-love.

Farewell to you, my lady-love! Farewell, mistress on account of
your deed, my lady-love!

Retort

O friends! I will now ask you about my love.

Where has my love gone, my love who is singing against me?

I ask you, who walks with my love.

Oh, where is my love, where is the love that I had for my love?

For I feel, really feel, foolish, because I acted foolishly against my
love.

For what I did caused people to laugh at me on account of what I
did to you, my love.

For I am despised on account of my love for you, my true love,
for you, my love.

For you have said that you will live in Knight Inlet.

Oh, Knight Inlet is far away, for that is the name of the place where
my love is going.

Oh, Rivers Inlet is far away, for that is the name of the place where
my love is going.

For he forgot of my love, my true love.

For in vain he goes about trying to find someone who will love
him as I did, my love.

Don't try to leave me without turning back to my love, my love.

Oh, my love, turn back to your slave, who preserved your life.

I am downcast, and I cry for the love of my love.

But my life is killed by the words of my love.

Good-by, my love, my past true-love!

The passing of a loved one—the inspiration for many great elegies
among the European races—was seldom an occasion for Indian lyrics.
No doubt the Indian felt his loss as poignantly as we might do, but
his attitude toward death and the hereafter was so entirely different
from Christian concepts that a personal expression of grief was a rare
thing in Indian poetry. Formal ritual songs addressed to the spirits
of the dead are found, such as the "Prayer to a Dead Wife" given

Tlingits used oratory for this, not poems!

in Chapter 4, but it is hard to find any real laments except among the Aztecs of Mexico and our singers of the Northwest Coast.

Here is the song of a Tlingit man mourning for his father and uncle:

THE NATION'S DRUM HAS FALLEN DOWN [194]

The nation's drum has fallen down, my mother.
Take the drum out from among the nations so that they can hear
my mother.

Another from this tribe was composed by Small-Lake-Underneath, about a drifting log found full of nails, out of which a house was built. It was sung at a mourning feast. The "log" metaphor was apparently original with the singer.

MOURNING SONG [194]

I always compare you to a drifting log with iron nails in it.
Let my brother float in, in that way.
Let him float ashore on a good sandy beach.
I always compare you, my mother, to the sun passing behind the
clouds.
That is what makes the world dark.

The third of these Tlingit songs is quite lyrical in tone. It was composed by Among-the-Brant when his wife had been taken from him, and he felt very sad. In the original language, the last line was given in the dialect of a neighboring tribe, the Tsimshian.

CARRYING MY MIND AROUND [194]

My own mind is very hard to me.
It is just as if I were carrying my mind around.
What is the matter with you?

A curious mourning song comes from Vancouver Island. Modana and his sister were drowned on Virgin Rock, and the song was chanted by all the men and women in the house of the dead ones. The tribal government of the Kwakiutl, it should be explained, is in the hands of secret societies, most important of which was the Cannibal Society, of which Modana was a member.

MOURNING SONG FOR MODANA [19]

Ye he he ya! It deprived me of my mind, when the moon went
down at the edge of the waters. *Ye he he ya!*

Ye he he ya! It deprived me of my breath, when the mouse-dancer
began to gnaw on the water. *Ye he he ya!*

Ye he he ya! It deprived me of my mind when Modana began to
utter the cannibal-cry on the water. *Ye he he ya!*

Interesting also is a "love-song of the dead" from the same tribe:

LOVE-SONG OF THE DEAD [19]

You are hard-hearted against me, you are hard-hearted against me,
my dear, *ha ha ye ha ha ha!*

You are cruel against me, you are cruel against me, my dear, *ha ha
ye ha ha ha!*

For I am tired waiting for you to come here, my dear, *ha ha ye
ha ha ha!*

Now I shall cry differently on your account, my dear, *ha ha ye
ha ha ha!*

Ah, I shall go down to the lower world, there I shall cry for you,
my dear, *ha ha ye ha ha ha!*

Satire among the Tlingit and Kwakiutl is more heavy-handed than
that we have noted among the Eskimos. Among the Klamath tribes-
men of Oregon, however, brief songs with an epigrammatic power
worthy of the Greek Anthology have been written down by
Gatschet.[100] Many of these concern courtship and love. The Indian
maiden asks: "And when will you pay for me a wedding gift?" and
the scornful lad ungallantly replies: "A canoe I'll give for you half
filled with water!" Less veiled in its sarcasm is another dialog. The
girl says: "Young man, I will not love you, for you run around with
no blanket on. I do not desire such a husband." The boy replies:
"And I do not like a frog-shaped woman with swollen eyes." When
one remembers that wives were often purchased among the Indians
in exchange for riding horses, the following commentary on a
lady's beauty has quite the savor of Martial: "Slow-running horses
he paid for his wife." Another brief song of ridicule suggests im-
proper behavior on the part of an old Klamath spinster: "White

geese saw an old woman hiding, saw an old maid hiding in the grass." And this proverb-like song satirizes feminine voracity at meals: "When the female wolf has devoured the elk-buck she cries for more."

Subtlety of this sort, or the sharp satire of the Eskimo drum-song, was not found in the song contests of the Pacific Northwest tribes. Vituperation and boasting about one's wealth in goods were the main marks of these contests. Both the Tlingit and the Kwakiutl engaged in feasts called "potlatches" (Chinook jargon, from the Chinook word *patshatl*, "giving"). On these occasions the head of one rich family tried to outdo a rival by public displays of property. Indian society of the Pacific Coast was stratified into three classes: chiefs or nobles, common people, and slaves. The mark of a chief was his ancestry and the amount of vulgar wealth he could display. Personal names were chosen to reveal this greatness—names like Throwing-Away-Property, Making-Potlatch-Dances-All-the-Time, and Too-Rich. Pride of a family, which centered about the clan crests of birds or animals seen carved on their totem poles, had to be shown by extravagant gestures of what was supposed to seem like insane generosity in giving away possessions. Chiefs therefore publicly vied in bestowing wealth upon each other. Actually, little was risked, because the reluctant recipient of a gift had to return it, with interest, or suffer shame. The wealth paraded was in the form of "coppers," shield-shaped plates of crude metal upon which the totem of the owner was scratched. These plates had names of their own and were valued at various prices in terms of trade blankets. They were offered at a kind of truculent auction ceremony in which by long speeches and songs the owner of the copper pictured himself as a native Croesus whose wealth dazzled the eyes of the whole world. In the old days, a chief would sometimes bash in the heads of a few slaves (which were also property) to show his excessive wealth.

The following boasting song was sung by New-Rich, chief of the Auk people of the Tlingits, who had defeated a Yakutat chief in a potlatch contest. It implies that his rival owned no real coppers and tried to pawn off cedar-bark counterfeits instead.

SONG OF NEW-RICH [194]

I am very much ashamed of the chief.
He only made a pretense with cedar bark.
He made it into copper plates.
Will you come back here?
Do you think we never have feasts in this town?

A song of boasting, also from the Tlingits, indulges in heavy slander:

ANGRY SONG [194]

Little Raven, I hate what you keep saying, because you are a slave's son and can see nothing.

I hate to have you talk to me because you have spots all over your face like a big sea cucumber and look like a slave.

Don't you know that, because you can not see anything, you big slave's son, you keep picking up sand instead of dipping into the dish?

A final potlatch song comes from the Kwakiutl:

SONG OF QWAXILA [19]

I am the only great tree, I the chief! I am the only great tree, I the chief! You here are right under me, tribes! You are my younger brothers under me, tribes! You sit in the middle of the rear of the house, tribes! You surround me like a fence, tribes! I am your Eagle, tribes! *Ya, he ā, ā, ye, ya!*

I wish you would bring your counter of property, tribes, that he may in vain try to count what is going to be given away by the great copper-maker, the chief. *Ya, ye, ā, ā!*

Go on! Raise the unattainable potlatch-pole, for this is the only thick tree, the only thick root of the tribes. *Ya, ye, ā, ā!*

Now our chief will become angry in the house, he will perform the dance of anger. Our chief will perform the dance of fury. I shall suffer the short-life maker of our chief. *Ya, ye, ā, ā!*

I only laugh at him, I sneer at him who empties [the boxes] in his house, his potlatch-house, and the inviting-house that is the cause of hunger. All the house-dishes are in the greatest house of our chief. *Ya, ye, ā, ā!*

The Indians of the Northwest, like all other Indians, were fond of their children and indulged them to a point just short of spoiling them. Mothers quieted their children by singing, just as all mothers do, and no one needs to be a specialist in the interpretation of poetry to be able to enjoy the cradle-songs of the American Indians. Lullabies in all languages are pretty much alike. The best of the children's songs that have been translated come from the Northwest and from the Pueblo dwellers of the Southwest (see Chapter 4).

Here are two cradle-songs from the Tlingit:

CRADLE-SONG FOR A BOY [194]

Let me shoot a small bird for my younger brother.
Let me spear a small trout for my sister.

CRADLE-SONG FOR A GIRL [194]

If I do not take anything [to the party], I shall be ashamed,
    I shall be ashamed.
Little girls, listen. Little girls, listen.

A charming cradle-song comes from the Haida tribe of the Queen Charlotte Islands. The child is asked, "Whence have you fallen?"—that is, "How did you come here to us?"

HAIDA CRADLE-SONG [191]

Whence have you fallen, have you fallen? Whence have you
    fallen, have you fallen?
Did you fall, fall, fall, fall, from the top of the salmon-berry
    bushes?

These two songs for parents to use in awakening their children and reminding them of tasks to be done come from the Kwakiutl. The little boy should arise and go hunting; the little girl should go to the beach and dig for clams.

SONG OF PARENTS WHO WANT TO WAKE UP THEIR SON [19]

Don't sleep! for your paddle fell into the water, and your spear.
Don't sleep! for the ravens and crows are flying about.

SONG OF PARENTS WHO WANT TO WAKE UP THEIR DAUGHTER [19]

Don't sleep too much! Your digging-stick fell into the water, and your basket.
Wake up! It is nearly low water. You will be late down on the beach.

Another such song, interesting for stylistic reasons, has already been given in Chapter 1 during an explanation of repetition with variations.

A cradle-song which, like the preceding two, was chanted in a sort of Indian "baby-talk," is supposed to have been sung by a Kwakiutl chief's daughter, proud of her lineage and wealth. The "coppers" mentioned are, of course, those sheets of useless but ostentatious property that a chief was supposed to bestow freely to show his power.

SONG OF CHIEF'S DAUGHTER [19]

Be ready, O chiefs! sons of the tribes! to be my husbands; for I come to make my husband a great chief through my father, for I am mistress, *ha ha aya ha ha aya!*
I, mistress, come to be your wife, O princes of the chiefs of the tribes! I am seated on coppers, and have many names and privileges that will be given by my father to my future husband, *ha ha aya ha ha aya!*
For my belt has been woven by my mother, which I use when I look after the dishes that will be given as a marriage present by my father to him who shall be my husband, when many kinds of food shall be given in the marriage-feast by my father to him who shall be my husband, *ha ha aya ha ha aya!*

From the Makah tribe of Cape Flattery comes this little song to a baby boy:

MAKAH LULLABY [54, 69]

My little son,
You will put a whale harpoon and a sealing spear into your canoe,
Not knowing what use you will make of them.

≳ 4 ≲

DESERT DWELLERS OF THE SOUTHWEST

THE RICHEST hunting grounds for contemporary seekers of Indian poetry have been the arid lands of southwestern United States and northern Mexico. In this quarter of the continent many tribes can be found who still live much as they did four hundred years ago, when Francisco Vásquez Coronado and his band of Spanish adventurers marched north from Mexico City and explored from California to Kansas, living for two years in the walled villages of the natives that still bear the name of Pueblo Indians.

This region, where a burning sun, a turquoise sky, and sudden massing rain-clouds determine the daily mode of life of the dwellers in the dry, canyon-gashed landscape, has been occupied for thousands of years, and in it developed the highest level of civilization north of the Valley of Mexico. The chief needs of those who found refuge there were food, water, and security. The few spots along watercourses where these needs could be supplied were subjected to frequent invasions (at least five main language groups are found in the area, representing waves of migration at different times). The lack of easily hunted animals or many edible wild plants forced the inhabitants to settle down and become farmers. Agricultural life led to the building of permanent houses, gave opportunity for the

59

creation of a domestic village society, permitted the storing up of food and other forms of wealth, and provided leisure to create works of art and to develop an intricate ritual of worship. The wealth of the Pueblos attracted raiding nomads who often in turn adopted their sedentary culture. When we first consider this large culture area, we are tempted to make a strong distinction between the dwellers in walled towns and the roving tribes who lived off the country; actually, when the effect of long exposure to the southwest environment is taken into account, it turns out that the typical culture of the area is that of the oldest inhabitants, the Pueblos, and that tribes on the fringe of the Pueblo region approached this type but showed modifications resulting from contact with mountain or plains customs.

The key traits of Pueblo culture may be listed as cultivation of regular crops, erection of plastered and timbered dwellings of masonry or sun-baked clay, use of the metate or corn-grinding stone rather than the mortar, high ability in producing loom-woven fabric and color-decorated pottery, and, above all, an intense ritualism revealed in lengthy, often archaic chants and songs of sequence.

The unique villages of the medieval predecessors of the Pueblos, who flourished from the tenth to the fifteenth centuries, were made up of numerous cell-like adjoining rooms. These terraced pre-Columbian apartment houses were often of immense size; one cluster in old Pecos had 517 rooms, and another 585. The Coronado expedition in 1541 and 1542 discovered the inheritors of this culture in more than seventy towns in what is now northern Arizona and New Mexico, having in all a population of twenty thousand souls. Among the Pueblos, woven garments of cultivated cotton were worn (the men did the weaving), but skin clothing and leather moccasins and leggings were also found; buffalo robes obtained by trade with the hunting tribes to the east were prized. Corn, beans, and squash were the main dishes, but pine nuts were gathered and pounded into meal; the turkey was domesticated, not for food, but for its feathers. The turquoise was mined and used as decoration. Social grouping was complex. Each village was independent, although temporary war alliances were made. The village elected a governor and a war chief.

There were two sets of priests, one for summer and one for winter. There were many societies and cults which sponsored dramatic ceremonies; the circular underground kiva or fraternity chamber of the men was an important part of the village. All their arts—and every pueblo dweller was an artist—were reflections of a spirit of gratitude for the life-giving forces of earth and sky. The great communal art was that of the dance—the Rain Dance of Sía and the Snake Dance of the Hopis (which was also a rain dance) are best known. These dramas were accompanied by the music of pipes and drums, were performed in ceremonial garments and symbolic masks, and were prefaced by the making of priest-drawn "sand paintings" of vivid pigments and ground meal.

The main centers of Pueblo culture in historic times have been among the Zuñi of "Cibola" on the Arizona-New Mexico border, the first discovered group and the one whose poetry has been most intensively studied; the Hopi of northern Arizona; the high mesa citadel of Acoma, east of Zuñi; and the villages of the upper Rio Grande, from Taos south to Isleta.

The Navahos of New Mexico and Arizona are an example of a barbaric, raiding band which since the coming of the white man has settled down and become one of the most progressive tribes in the land; their numbers have actually increased under civilized conditions. They have shown an aptitude for clever cultural borrowing: the weaving of their famed woolen rugs they learned from their neighbors the Hopis; their carefully pastured tribal wealth consists of sheep and horses, which they obtained from the Spanish and Mexicans to the south; they learned the Mexican art of the silversmith, and became good metal workers, as every tourist knows. They do not take to town life, however, and still dwell in the "hogan," a hive-shaped log shelter that may be found scattered about their large reservations. As a tribe they have now become not too markedly different in behavior from the Pueblo groups. Their intense ritualism is expressed in the lengthy chants which enact their tribal myths.

The Apache, a widely scattered number of bands, were also raiding nomads even a few generations ago, when the names of Cochise, Victorio, and Geronimo brought fear to the settlements. Their culture, especially in the tribes to the west, approached that of the Pueblos, but the eastern Apaches remind one of the Plains type, for they lived in tepees, gathered wild food plants, made baskets, acquired horses, and followed the buffalo. Formerly they ranged from Oklahoma and Texas west to the Colorado River; they are now settled on reservations. The main divisions are the Jicarilla, Mescalero, San Carlos, White Mountain, and Chiricahua.

The Pimas of the Arizona border country show a group transitional toward the Pueblos. They used to build adobe houses and practice irrigation, but placed more dependence upon wild plants such as the mesquite and the cactus; they, like the Pueblos, raised and wove cotton, and made excellent baskets. The Papagos, their kindred, were still less advanced. On a fairly low cultural level also were the tribes of the lower Colorado. When one visits the desert regions where all these tribes have managed to live for centuries, he is usually struck with surprise that any human being could exist at all on this barren soil.

Many kinds of songs are found in the Southwest, particularly ceremonial chants, prayers, magical incantations, medicine songs, and war songs. A few love songs, children's songs, game songs, and social dance songs have also been found. Many good translators have worked in this area: among these should be mentioned Natalie Curtis for the Navaho and for the Keresan village of Laguna; Herbert J. Spinden for the Tewa or Tehua, five villages of Tanoan stock on the Rio Grande north of Santa Fe; Matilda Coxe Stevenson for the Keresan village of Sía; Ruth Bunzel for the Zuñi group; Washington Matthews for the Navaho, among whom Cosmos Mindeleff and Harry Hoijer have also found material for translation; Frank Russell for the Pima; Frances Densmore for the Papago and Yuma Indians; and Pliny E. Goddard for the Apaches. Except for the Yumas, whose songs have few words or none, the Colorado River tribes have contributed little to the store of translated poetry. The songs of the California Indians still remain to be studied.

Ritual poetry reached a high development in the Southwest. This kind of verse, designed for religious, ceremonial, or magical use, was ordinarily highly formal in style, was sung or recited on specific occasions connected with tribal feasts, worship, prayer, or curative rites, and was commonly voiced by priests, shamans, or medicine men, although the layman might sing incantations to insure success in horse-breeding, hunting, or corn-growing. We should remember that what we call "magic" was to the Indian the best science he could muster, for he used it in an attempt to gain control of his environment for his own purposes. Knowing that he himself was swayed to imitate the example of others, he saw nothing incongruous in performing acts which he hoped the gods of nature would imitate and thus bring the needed rain, or assist in the drawing away of disease, or encourage fertility in plants and animals. The ideas of the shamans were, then, based on the theories of sympathetic magic which for centuries were behind the common practices of all mankind.

Some of the finest American Indian poetry is to be found in the great ritual ceremonials of the various tribes. These religious observances—some of which extended over many days and in which the entire tribe took part—form the only sort of Indian poetry which may be called dramatic in the sense of being comparable to our stage plays or pageants. True, there existed among the Pueblos certain societies such as the *koshare* or "delight-makers," whose business it was to perform clownish antics at certain festivals; but their performances were unrehearsed and have not been extensively recorded. The dramatic *katzina* songs of the Hopi tribe were, of course, associated with the tribal religious beliefs. The masked dancers of other southwestern tribes also represented the gods come back to earth, incarnated in ritualistic symbol and song, to mingle with men and share in their joys and labors. Therefore if we wish to find any evidence of the origins of dramatic poetry among the Indians, we must seek it—as we seek it in ancient Greek literature and in early English literature in the miracle plays—among the religious ceremonials.

One of the great monuments of Indian poetry in English is the dramatic "Mountain Chant" of the Navahos, translated by Dr. Washington Matthews and published in 1887. This ceremony consisted in the enactment of tribal myths, which form the sequential key for interpolated songs. The "Mountain Chant" has thirteen episodes comprising 161 songs; the sequence having the largest num-

ber of songs runs to twenty-six, and the least number in a sequential
series is seven. Only a few of these many songs have been translated.
At appropriate times in the ceremony, these "songs of sequence"
were introduced as interludes. The following is a good example
of one of these songs:

FIRST SONG OF DAWN BOY [144]

Where my kindred dwell,
    There I wander.
The Red Rock house,
    There I wander.
Where dark *kethawns* [sacred sticks]
    are at the doorway,
    There I wander.
At the *yuni* [seat of honor] the striped
    cotton hangs with pollen.
    There I wander.
Going around with it.
    There I wander.
Taking another, I depart with it.
    With it I wander.
In the house of long life,
    There I wander.
In the house of happiness,
    There I wander.
Beauty before me,
    With it I wander.
Beauty behind me,
    With it I wander.
Beauty below me,
    With it I wander.
Beauty above me,
    With it I wander.
Beauty all around me,
    With it I wander.
In old age traveling,
    With it I wander.
On the beautiful trail I am,
    With it I wander.

Here are two thunder songs from the "Mountain Chant":

FIRST SONG OF THE THUNDER [144]

Thonah! Thonah!
There is a voice above,
The voice of the thunder.
Within the dark cloud,
Again and again it sounds,
Thonah! Thonah!

Thonah! Thonah!
There is a voice below,
The voice of the grasshopper.
Among the plants,
Again and again it sounds,
Thonah! Thonah!

TWELFTH SONG OF THE THUNDER [144]

The voice that beautifies the land!
The voice above,
The voice of the thunder.
Within the dark cloud
Again and again it sounds,
The voice that beautifies the land.

The voice that beautifies the land!
The voice below:
The voice of the grasshopper.
Among the plants
Again and again it sounds,
The voice that beautifies the land.

In these verses there is an intricate use of slight but effective variations in parallel construction, and both songs are parallel to each other. These poems strike one as excellent English which is yet very close to the original.

The "Night Chant," another Navaho ceremony, contains no less than twenty-four sequences with a total of 324 songs. Some of these are powerful in symbolism—the "Night Chant" is the great healing ceremony of the Navaho tribe—and although most of the inter-

polated chants cannot be truly appreciated unless the reader under-
stands their place in the dramatic representation of the medicine-
myths, a few of these songs of sequence may easily stand alone as
examples of authentic and charming Indian poetry. In the following
bluebird song, Matthews has chosen to replace the Indian name of
the bird with the Latin name of the genus.

DAYLIGHT SONG [145]

He has a voice, he has a voice.
Just at daylight Sialia calls.
The bluebird has a voice,
He has a voice, his voice melodious,
His voice melodious, that flows in gladness.
Sialia calls, Sialia calls.

He has a voice, he has a voice.
Just at twilight Sialia calls.
The bird *tsolgali* has a voice,
He has a voice, his voice melodious,
His voice melodious, that flows in gladness.
Sialia calls, Sialia calls.

From the same ceremonial comes a song of one of the Navaho gods:

A SONG OF NAYENZGANI [145]

I am the Slayer of the Alien Gods.
Where'er I roam,
Before me
Forests white are strewn around.
The lightning scatters;
But 'tis I who cause it.

I am the Child of the Water.
Where'er I roam,
Behind me
Waters white are strewn around.
The tempest scatters;
But 'tis I who cause it.

The migrant Navaho people, even more than many primitive
groups, were concerned to explain the origins of their tribe and

their place in creation. This is the song that was chanted by the god Bekotsidi to bless the animals that he was shaping during the Navaho genesis:

THE SONG OF BEKOTSIDI [145]

Now Bekotsidi, that am I. For them I make.
Now child of Day Bearer am I. For them I make.
Now Day Bearer's beam of blue. For them I make.
Shines on my feet and your feet too. For them I make.
Horses of all kinds now increase. For them I make.
At my fingers' tips and yours. For them I make.
Beasts of all kinds now increase. For them I make.
The bluebirds now increase. For them I make.
Soft goods of all kinds now increase. For them I make.
Now with the pollen they increase. For them I make.
Increasing now, they will last forever. For them I make.
In old age wandering on the trail of beauty. For them I make.
To form them fair, for them I labor. For them I make.

Half a century after Matthews made his studies, phonograph recordings were made of songs of the Navaho creation myth, as sung by a native medicine man, Hasteen Klah. These have been translated by Dr. Harry Hoijer and edited by Dr. George Herzog. Among the best of these creation-myth songs may be found the following four:

SONG OF THE FLOOD [131]

The first man—you are his child, he is your child.
The first woman—you are his child, he is your child.
The water monster—you are his child, he is your child.
The black sea-horse—you are his child, he is your child.
The black snake—you are his child, he is your child.
The big blue snake—you are his child, he is your child.
The white corn—you are his child, he is your child.
The yellow corn—you are his child, he is your child.
The corn pollen—you are his child, he is your child.
The corn beetle—you are his child, he is your child.
Sahanahray—you are his child, he is your child.
Bekayhozhon—you are his child, he is your child.

The Navaho words in the last two lines have esoteric significance.

SONG OF THE SUN AND MOON [131]

The first man holds it in his hands,
He holds the sun in his hands.
In the center of the sky, he holds it in his hands.
As he holds it in his hands, it starts upward.

The first woman holds it in her hands,
She holds the moon in her hands.
In the center of the sky, she holds it in her hands.
As she holds it in her hands, it starts upward.

The first man holds it in his hands,
He holds the sun in his hands.
In the center of the sky, he holds it in his hands.
As he holds it in his hands, it starts downward.

The first woman holds it in her hands,
She holds the moon in her hands.
In the center of the sky, she holds it in her hands.
As she holds it in her hands, it starts downward.

THERE ARE NO PEOPLE SONG [131]

You say there were no people.
   Smoke was spreading [over the earth].
You say there were no people.
   Smoke was spreading.

First Man was the very first to emerge, they say,
   Smoke was spreading.
He brought with him the various robes and precious things, they say,
   Smoke was spreading.
He brought with him the white corn and the yellow corn, they say,
   Smoke was spreading.
He brought with him the various animals and the growing things,
   they say,
      Smoke was spreading.

   You say there were no people.
      Smoke was spreading.

First Woman was the very first to emerge, they say,
   Smoke was spreading.

She brought with her the various precious things and robes, they say,
      Smoke was spreading.
She brought with her the yellow corn and the varicolored corn,
    they say,
      Smoke was spreading.
She brought with her the various animals and the growing things,
    they say,
      Smoke was spreading.

    You say there were no people.
      Smoke was spreading.
    You say there were no people.
      Smoke was spreading.

SONG OF COYOTE WHO STOLE THE FIRE [131]

I am frivolous Coyote; I wander around.
I have seen the Black God's fire; I wander around.
I stole his fire from him; I wander around.
I have it! I have it!

I am changing Coyote; I wander around.
I have seen the bumble-bee's fire; I wander around.
I stole his fire from him; I wander around.
I have it! I have it!

With these Navaho examples of emergence themes may be compared the following archaic Pima "creation song" describing the making of the earth. It was translated by Frank Russell.

THE CREATION OF THE EARTH [172]

    Earth Magician shapes this world.
      Behold what he can do!
    Round and smooth he molds it.
      Behold what he can do!
    Earth Magician makes the mountains.
      Heed what he has to say!
    He it is that makes the mesas.
      Heed what he has to say.
    Earth Magician shapes this world;
      Earth Magician makes its mountains;

Makes all larger, larger, larger.
  Into the earth the Magician glances;
Into its mountains he may see.

Prayers of a ritual sort were a part of religion in the Southwest.
When white men first discovered the Zuñi pueblos, the Spanish
soldiers quickly noticed that at dawn the tribal priests or *pekwin*
recited prayers before the people. "They have priests who preach
to them, whom they call *papas*," wrote one of the chroniclers of the
Coronado expedition. "These are the elders. They go up on the
highest roof of the village and preach to the village from there, like
public criers, in the morning while the sun is rising, the whole
village being silent and sitting in the galleries to listen. They tell
them how they are to live, and I believe that they give certain
commandments for them to keep." It happens that the prayers of
this particular tribe have been extensively studied by Ruth Bunzel,
and from her monograph several ritual prayers will be given—
prayers which probably have changed little in form since Coronado's
conquest.

These prayers are fixed rites rather than spontaneous inventions,
and there are a large number to fit various occasions. Says the trans-
lator: "Prayer in Zuñi is not a spontaneous outpouring of the heart.
It is rather the repetition of a fixed formula. Only in such prayers
as those accompanying individual offerings of corn meal and food
is a certain amount of individual variation possible, and even here
variation is restricted to the matter of abridgment or inclusiveness.
The general form of the prayer, the phraseology and the nature of
the request, conform strictly to types for other prayers." [30] The
prayers are learned in the underground kivas, and boys learn the
proper prayers from their fathers. Some prayers which are rare,
secret, or supposed to have great power are highly valuable in
monetary terms, and may be sold by their possessors.

The following is a brief prayer to the sun at dawn:

ZUÑI PRAYER AT SUNRISE [32]

Now this day,
My sun father,

Now that you have come out standing to your sacred place,
That from which we draw the water of life,
Prayer meal,
Here I give to you.
Your long life,
Your old age,
Your waters,
Your seeds,
Your riches,
Your power,
Your strong spirit,
All these to me may you grant.

The next Zuñi prayer accompanied the offering of prayer sticks to the sacred ancestors at each full moon.

OFFERING OF PRAYER STICKS [32]

This many are the days
Since our moon mother
Yonder in the west
Appeared still small.
When she became fully grown
Seeking yonder along the river courses
The ones who are our fathers,
Male willow,
Female willow,
Four times cutting the straight young shoots,
To my house,
I brought my road.

This day,
With my warm human hands
I took hold of them.
I gave my plume wands human form
With the striped cloud tail
Of the one who is my grandfather,
The male turkey
With the eagle's thin cloud tail,
With the striped cloud wings
And massed cloud tails

Of all the birds of summer,
With these four times I gave my plume wands human form.
With the flesh of the one who is my mother,
Cotton woman,
Even a poorly made cotton thread,
Four times encircling them and tying it about their bodies,
I gave the plume wands human form.
With the flesh of the one who is our mother,
Black paint woman,
Four times covering them with flesh,
I gave my plume wands human form.

In a short time the plume wands were ready.
Taking the plume wands,
I made my road go forth.
Yonder with prayers
We took our road.
Thinking, "Let it be here,"
Our earth mother
We passed upon her road.
Our fathers,
There on your earth mother,
There where you are waiting your plume wands
We have passed you on your roads.
There where you are all gathered together in beauty
Now that you are to receive your plume wands,
You are gathered together.

This day I give you plume wands.
By means of your supernatural wisdom
You will clothe yourself with the plume wands.
Wherever you abide permanently,
Your little wind-blown cloud,
Your thin wisps of cloud,
Your hanging stripes of cloud,
Your massed up clouds, replete with living waters,
You will send forth to stay with us.
They will come out standing on all sides.
With your fine rain caressing the earth,

With your weapons, the lightning,
With your rumbling thunder,
Your great crashes of thunder,
With your fine rain caressing the earth,
Your heavy rain caressing the earth,
With your great pile of waters here at Itiwana,
With these you will pass us on our roads;
In order that you may come to us thus
I have given you plume wands.

My fathers,
When you have taken your plume wands,
With your waters,
Your seeds,
Your riches,
Your power,
Your strong spirit,
With all your good fortune whereof you are possessed,
Me you will bless.

The following prayer is unique, according to the translator, because it is the only one she discovered which was addressed to an individual; even here, the ancestors are mentioned. It is a prayer to a dead wife, after the four-day period of rigorous mourning. The person addressed as "You, my mother" is in reality the wife—it is a term used thus for one's wife or child in moments of great tenderness. It should be noted that this poem is a ritual formula, and not a personalized elegy. Part of the purpose of the prayer is to protect the living from the haunting pull of the dead soul.

PRAYER TO A DEAD WIFE [32]

Even so may it be.
Now this day,
My ancestors,
You have attained the far-off place of waters [land of the dead].
This day,
Carrying plume wands,
Plume wands which I have prepared for your use,
I pass you on your roads.

I offer you plume wands.
When you have taken my plume wands,
All your good fortune whereof you are possessed
You will grant to me.
And furthermore
You, my mother,
Verily, in the daylight
With thoughts embracing,
We passed our days.
Now you have attained the far-off place of waters.
I give you plume wands,
Plume wands which I have prepared for your use.
Drawing your plume wands to you,
And sharing my plume wands.

Indeed, under no conditions shall you take anyone away.*

Among all the corn priests' ladder-descending children,
All the little boys,
The little girls,
And those whose roads go ahead,
Was one, perhaps even a valuable man,
Who, his heart becoming angry because of something,
Injured you with his power.†

That one only you will think to drag down.

All of your good fortune whatsoever
May you grant to us.
Preserving us along a safe road.
May our roads be fulfilled.

This ritual prayer of the Navaho tribe comes from the "Mountain Chant" already described:

---

* "The dead are lonely without the living and try to draw them away. The wife longs for her living husband, the mother for her children. Therefore these individuals stand in grave danger of death."—Translator's note.

† This refers to the evil person whose enmity caused the mortal illness of the wife. The prayer seeks to turn the baleful influence of death upon the person who caused that death.

INVOCATION TO DSILYI N'EYANI [141]

Reared Within the Mountains!
Lord of the Mountains!
Young Man!
Chieftain!
I have made your sacrifice.
I have prepared a smoke for you.
My feet restore thou for me.
My legs restore thou for me.
My body restore thou for me.
My mind restore thou for me.
My voice thou restore for me.
Restore all for me in beauty.
Make beautiful all that is before me.
Make beautiful all that is behind me.
It is done in beauty.
It is done in beauty.
It is done in beauty.
It is done in beauty.

Ritual formulas were developed by most Indian tribes to accompany many acts of daily life, as well as to enforce the power of magical incantations and healing charms. What Miss Bunzel has written of the Zuñi practices would hold true in general for many North American tribes: "Many ritual acts are accompanied by song. There are special song sequences for setting up and taking down altars, for mixing medicine water or soapsuds, for bathing the head at initiations, to accompany various acts of curing. These are all special songs of the curing societies. Like prayers, they must be learned ritualistically. They are in the nature of incantations; many of them are in foreign languages or have no intelligible words. In addition to these songs of the medicine societies, there are many individually owned songs of magical power, especially songs for planting, for 'dancing the corn'; individual medicine songs, or songs associated with personal amulets. Certain women also have grinding songs in addition to the well-known songs of the men." [30] Many good incantations are found in the Southwest: for rain-making, for house dedications, for horse-breeding, for hunting, and for corn-planting and corn-grinding. There are also many medicine songs for curing ceremonies.

The importance of seasonal rains to the Indians dependent upon crops for their food supply is indicated by many rain rituals. This invocation from the Tewa pueblos, translated by Spinden, offers imagery which refers to the sky as a blanket-weaving loom.

SONG OF THE SKY LOOM [186]

O our Mother the Earth, O our Father the Sky,
Your children are we, and with tired backs
We bring you the gifts that you love.
Then weave for us a garment of brightness;
May the warp be the white light of morning,
May the weft be the red light of evening,
May the fringes be the falling rain,
May the border be the standing rainbow.
Thus weave for us a garment of brightness
That we may walk fittingly where birds sing,
That we may walk fittingly where grass is green,
O our Mother the Earth, O our Father the Sky!

From the Keresan village of Sía comes this invocation, translated by Mrs. Stevenson:

RAIN SONG OF THE GIANT SOCIETY [188]

Middle of the world below,
Door of *shipapo* [entrance
    to lower world],
My medicine is precious,
It is as my heart.
Arrow of Lightning,
Come to us,
Hear the echo.
Who is it?
Spruce of the North.
All your people,
Your thoughts,
Come to us. ,
Who is it?

White Floating Clouds.
Your thoughts
Come to us,
All your people,
Your thoughts,
Come to us.
Who is it?
Clouds Like the Plains.
Your thoughts
Come to us.
Who is it?
Arrow of Lightning.
Your thoughts
Come to us.
Who is it?
Earth Horizon.
All your people,
Your thoughts,
Come to us.

Another ceremonial song begging for rain represents the Pima
tribe and was translated by Frank Russell:

PIMA RAIN SONG [172]

Hi-ihiya naiho-o! Pluck out the feathers
　　From the wing of the Eagle and turn them
Toward the east where lie the large clouds.
　　Hitciya yahina-a! Pluck out the soft down
From the breast of the Eagle and turn it
　　Toward the west where sail the small clouds.
Hitciya yahina! Beneath the abode
　　Of the rain gods it is thundering;
Large corn is there. *Hitciya yahina!*
　　Beneath the abode of the rain gods
It is raining; small corn is there.

A song for the dedication of a new home, translated by Mindeleff,
comes from the Navaho:

HOUSE SONG TO THE EAST [147]

Far in the east, far below, there a house was made;
    Delightful house.
God of Dawn, there his house was made;
    Delightful house.
The Dawn, there his house was made;
    Delightful house.
White Corn, there its house was made;
    Delightful house.
Soft possessions, for them a house was made;
    Delightful house.
Water in plenty, surrounding, for it a house was made;
    Delightful house.
Corn pollen, for it a house was made;
    Delightful house.
The ancients make their presence delightful;
    Delightful house.

Before me, may it be delightful.
Behind me, may it be delightful.
Around me, may it be delightful.
Below me, may it be delightful.
Above me, may it be delightful.
All [universally], may it be delightful.

A ritual chant for the blessing and protection of the horse herds is found among the Navahos. Horses form one of the chief sources of tribal wealth; and the native breeder sings of the horses of Johano-Ai so that he, too, may have beautiful animals like those of the sun god. This song, and the imaginative legend behind it, must have been composed within the past four centuries, for previous to the coming of the Spaniards to the Southwest, the Indians had no horses and could not have invented this Phaeton-like legend in pre-Conquest days.

The god Johano-Ai, according to the tale, starts each day from his hogan in the east and rides to his hogan in the west, carrying the sun. He has five horses of different hues. When the weather is fair, he rides his turquoise horse or his horse of white shell or of pearl, but when the heavens are stormy, he is riding his horse of red shell or his horse of coal. Beneath the hoofs of the horses are spread precious hides or blankets. They are pastured on flower blossoms and given holy waters to drink from the four quarters of the world. When a horse of Johano-Ai gallops, he spurns up glittering grains of mineral dust such as that used in ceremonies; at other times he runs through a mist of sacred pollen. Standing among his herds, the Navaho scatters pollen and sings this ritual chant:

SONG OF THE HORSE [44]

How joyous his neigh!
Lo, the Turquoise Horse of Johano-Ai,
How joyous his neigh!
There on precious hides outspread standeth he;
How joyous his neigh.
There on tips of fair fresh flowers feedeth he;
How joyous his neigh.
There of mingled waters holy drinketh he;
How joyous his neigh.
There he spurneth dust of glittering grains;
How joyous his neigh.
There in mist of sacred pollen hidden, all hidden he;
How joyous his neigh.
There his offspring may grow and thrive for evermore;
How joyous his neigh!

A hunting song, also from the Navaho, is sung after the hunter has prayed to Hastyeyalti, god of sunrise and god of game. In the old days it was thought that if the hunter sat quite still and sang this song without mistake, the deer, charmed by the chant, would draw near enough to be shot through the heart.

In this song the hunter likens himself to the blackbird, beloved friend of the deer. He tells how the deer is drawn down the trail from the top of Black Mountain through the lush meadows, how he comes shyly through the dewy, pollen-laden flowers, and how, startled by the sight of the drawn bow, he turns to run, in vain.

HUNTING SONG [44]

Comes the deer to my singing,
Comes the deer to my song,
Comes the deer to my singing.

He, the blackbird, he am I,
Bird beloved of the wild deer.
Comes the deer to my singing.

From the Mountain Black,
From the summit,
Down the trail, coming, coming now,
Comes the deer to my singing.

Through the blossoms,
Through the flowers, coming, coming now,
Comes the deer to my singing.

Through the pollen, flower pollen,
Coming, coming now,
Comes the deer to my singing.

Starting with his left fore-foot,
Stamping, turns the frightened deer,
Comes the deer to my singing.

Quarry mine, blessed am I
In the luck of the chase.
Comes the deer to my singing.

Comes the deer to my singing,
Comes the deer to my song,
Comes the deer to my singing.

A second stanza follows, identical with the first except that the word "female" takes the place of "male," and the words "right fore-foot" take the place of "left fore-foot." The Navahos say that the male deer always starts with his left foot, and the doe with the right.

This brief invocation for good hunting comes from the Tewa pueblo of Nambé. "To come with dangling hands," explains Dr. Spinden, "is to come head down over the hunter's shoulder."

WITH DANGLING HANDS [186]

Come all game animals large,
Come all game animals small,
Hither come with dangling hands
To Nambé town! So now come all
To Nambé town with dangling hands!

Two deer-hunting songs from ceremonies of the San Carlos Apache tribe have been collected by Goddard:

DEER SONG [106]

At the south
Where the white shell ridges of the earth lie,
Where all kinds of fruit are ripe,
We two shall meet.

From there where the coral ridges of the earth lie,
We two will meet.
Where the ripe fruits are fragant,
We two will meet.

SONG OF THE DEER CEREMONY [106]

When the rising sun looks,
Walk out, they tell me.
When I went there, she who walks on the water was wild,
Her walk was wild, her eye was wild,
I came as she brought me some.

With a bone medicine belt not wild, I came to her.
With wind's footprints not wild, I came near her.
With a yellow spotted belt not wild, I came near her.
With a bone medicine shirt not wild, I came near her.

An interesting incantation for deer-stalking comes from the Zuñi tribe. "When a hunter sees deer tracks," Miss Bunzel explains, "he crouches down in the trail and offers prayer meal to the deer, with the request that he may reveal himself. The following text is taken from a folk tale in which success in hunting is the test imposed on suitors. Several suitors fail because they neglect to offer prayer meal to the prey."

PRAYER FOR STALKING DEER [32]

This day
He who holds our roads,
Our sun father,
Has come out standing to his sacred place.
Now that he has passed us on our roads,
Here we pass you on your road.
Divine one,
The flesh of the white corn,
Prayer meal,
Shell,
Corn pollen,
Here I offer to you.
With your wisdom
Taking the prayer meal,
The shell,
The corn pollen,
This day,
My fathers,
My mothers,
In some little hollow,
In some low brush,
You will reveal yourselves to me.
Then with your flesh,
With your living waters,
May I sate myself. In order that this may be
Here I offer you prayer meal.

Two ceremonial songs of the sacred corn come from two branches of the Apache tribe. Parallelism of thought, "rhyming of ideas," is found in the first of these, sung among the White Mountain Apaches:

CORN CEREMONY [107]

At the east where the black water lies stands the large corn, with staying roots, its large stalk, its red silk, its long leaves, its tassel dark and spreading, on which there is the dew.

At the sunset where the yellow water lies stands the large pumpkin with its tendrils, its long stem, its wide leaves, its yellow top on which there is pollen.

The following song is part of the Gotal ceremony of the Mescalero Apache, and is sung at dawn on the last day of the ritual. This ceremony at first glance is merely one of those very commonly used for the initiation of adolescent girls. "It is also," says Goddard, "a dramatic representation of the creation and of the annual and diurnal re-creations which come to the world."

A SONG OF GOTAL [104]

The black turkey-gobbler, under the East, the middle of his tail; toward us it is about to dawn.

The black turkey-gobbler, the tips of his beautiful tail; above us the dawn whitens.

The black turkey-gobbler, the tips of his beautiful tail; above us the dawn becomes yellow.

The sunbeams stream forward, dawn boys, with shimmering shoes of yellow;

On top of the sunbeams that stream toward us they are dancing.

At the East the rainbow moves forward, dawn maidens, with shimmering shoes and shirts of yellow dance over us.

Beautifully over us it is dawning.

Above us among the mountains the herbs are becoming green;

Above us on the tops of the mountains the herbs are becoming yellow.

Above us among the mountains, with shoes of yellow I go around the fruits and herbs that shimmer.

Above us among the mountains, the shimmering fruits with shoes and shirts of yellow are bent toward him.

On the beautiful mountains above it is daylight.

Here is a corn-planting ritual dance song from the Hopi tribe. The *katzinas*, represented by the doll-like fetishes found in Arizona curio shops, were intermediary deities who were supposed to transmit the prayers of the people to the high gods. "Long ago," explains Natalie Curtis, "the *Katzinas* lived upon the earth and danced in the plazas of the villages and brought the rain. But now they come no more, and so to bring the rain the Hopis themselves impersonate the *Katzinas*." The song is an excellent example of the stylistic feature of dual variation—yellow butterflies over the corn blossoms, blue butterflies over the bean blossoms.

KOROSTA KATZINA SONG [44]

Yellow butterflies,
Over the blossoming virgin corn,
With pollen-painted faces
Chase one another in brilliant throng.

Blue butterflies,
Over the blossoming virgin beans,
With pollen-painted faces
Chase one another in brilliant streams.

Over the blossoming corn,
Over the virgin corn,
Wild bees hum;
Over the blossoming beans,
Over the virgin beans,
Wild bees hum.

Over your field of growing corn
All day shall hang the thunder-cloud;
Over your field of growing corn
All day shall come the rushing rain.

A corn-grinding ritual chant made by the same translator comes
from the New Mexico pueblo of Laguna. The life-giving "wonder-
water" is the welcome rain water caught in hollows in the rocks
after a beneficent shower; it is "good medicine."

CORN-GRINDING SONG [44]

I-o-ho, wonder-water,
I-o-ho, wonder-water,
Life anew to him who drinks!
Look where southwest clouds are bringing rain;
Look where southeast clouds are bringing rain!
Life anew to him who drinks!
I-o-ho, wonder-water,
I-o-ho, wonder-water,
Life anew to him who drinks!

This "Discharming Song" from the initiation ceremony of a
women's society in the Hopi pueblo of Oraibi is a good example of a
pattern of repetition with deft variation:

DISCHARMING SONG [205]

To the North
  Discharm!
  Discharm!
  From the north
  Yellow buzzard,
  With the wing!

To the West
  Discharm!
  Discharm!
  From the west
  Green (blue) buzzard,
  With the wing!

To the South
  Discharm!
  Discharm!
  From the south
  Red buzzard,
  With the wing!

To the East
  Discharm!
  Discharm!
  From the east
  White buzzard,
  With the wing!

To the Northwest (above)
  Discharm!
  Discharm!
  From above
  Black buzzard,
  With the wing!

To the Southwest (below)
  Discharm!
  Discharm!
  From below
  Gray buzzard,
  With the wing!

Discharm!
Discharm!

Here is a sequence of corn-planting rituals from the Navaho, designed to invoke rain and rich harvests by the use of compulsive magic:

SONGS IN THE GARDEN OF THE HOUSE GOD [146]

Truly in the east
The white bean
And the great corn-plant
Are tied with the white lightning.
Listen! rain approaches!
The voice of the bluebird is heard.
Truly in the east
The white bean
And the great squash
Are tied with the rainbow.
Listen! rain approaches!
The voice of the bluebird is heard.

From the top of the great corn-plant the water gurgles, I hear it;
Around the roots the water foams, I hear it;
Around the roots of the plants it foams, I hear it;
From their tops the water foams, I hear it.

The corn grows up. The waters of the dark clouds drop, drop.
The rain descends. The waters from the corn leaves drop, drop.
The rain descends. The waters from the plants drop, drop.
The corn grows up. The waters of the dark mists drop, drop.

Shall I cull this fruit of the great corn-plant?
Shall you break it? Shall I break it?
Shall I break it? Shall you break it?
Shall I? Shall you?
Shall I cull this fruit of the great squash vine?
Shall you pick it up? Shall I pick it up?
Shall I pick it up? Shall you pick it up?
Shall I? Shall you?

The curative value of songs has always been highly considered by the Indians, and singing by the shaman usually forms an im-

portant part of the healing ceremony. In the words of the song there
is usually a reference to the source of the doctor's magical power—
often a bird or animal—and also a statement that the patient will
recover because of this curative power. With the following speci-
mens from the Southwest should be compared those from the
tribes given in other chapters.

This is the chant of Owl Woman, a medicine woman of the
Papago tribe, as she begins at dusk to fight for the life of a sick man
—a chant which she said was taught her by a spirit returned from
the dead:

MEDICINE SONG [54, 72]

How shall I begin my songs
In the blue night that is settling?

In the great night my heart will go out,
Toward me the darkness comes rattling.
In the great night my heart will go out.

Another charm, from the same tribe, is for the "Komotan sickness,"
which was supposed to affect warriors and unborn children:

THE SUNRISE [72]

The sun is rising,
At either side a bow is lying,
Beside the bows are lion-babies,
The sky is pink,
    That is all.

The moon is setting,
At either side are bamboos for arrow-making,
Beside the bamboos are wild-cat babies,
They walk uncertainly,
    That is all.

The following pair of brief medicine songs from the Yuma tribe of
the lower Colorado show scrutiny of nature:

THE WATER-BUG [54]

The water-bug is drawing the shadows of evening toward him
    across the water.

THE OWL [54]

The owl hooted and told of the morning star,
He hooted again and told of the dawn.

A number of Pima healing songs are given by Frank Russell. The
following "medicine song" was used to bring success in a deer hunt,
but was also supposed to be valuable in cases of sickness accompanied
by vomiting and dizziness. The "thornapple leaves" probably refer
to the jimson weed, poisonous to animals and man.

DATURA SONG [172]

At the time of the White Dawn
    At the time of the White Dawn,
I arose and went away.
    At Blue Nightfall I went away.

I ate the thornapple leaves
    And the leaves made me dizzy.
I drank the thornapple flowers
    And the drink made me stagger.

The hunter, Bow-Remaining,
    He overtook and killed me,
Cut and threw my horns away.
    The hunter, Reed-Remaining,
He overtook and killed me,
    Cut and threw my feet away.

Now the flies become crazy
    And they drop with flapping wings.
The drunken butterflies sit
    With opening and shutting wings.

A few more of these medicine songs will be given here. Like
similar songs from other tribes, they are laden with descriptions of
nature that reveal the natives' keen observation of their surround-
ings.

WIND SONG [172]

Wind now commences to sing;
    Wind now commences to sing.

The land stretches before me,
> Before me stretches away.

Wind's house now is thundering;
> Wind's house now is thundering.
I go roaring o'er the land,
> The land covered with thunder.

Over the windy mountains;
> Over the windy mountains,
Came the myriad-legged wind;
> The wind came running hither.

The Black Snake Wind came to me;
> The Black Snake Wind came to me,
Came and wrapped itself about,
> Came here running with its songs.

OWL SONG [172]

Towards the great Kámatuk mountain
> I go to join the singing,
During the glow of evening.
> I meet all the singers there.

Owl is singing in the distance,
> I hear him moving back and forth.
Many harlots came here running;
> Here came running and came laughing.

Small Owl resembles Tookot;
> The winds rise from Owl's feathers.
With their ashy tips he starts them.
> Small Owl is like the Large Owl.

Owl makes me drink the reddish water;
> Rapidly intoxicated
I try to walk straight toward the east,
> And find my footsteps staggering.

ROADRUNNER SONG [172]

Here is the red-eyed Roadrunner;
> Here is the red-eyed Roadrunner,

Who runs about the mistletoe.
  This is the red-eyed Roadrunner.

I run and hide! I run and hide!
  Now I kill the Gray Lizard
And I eat his fat body.
  I run and hide! I run and hide!

Over yonder in the mesquite
  Stands the Hawk's nest with its branches
Which rise like *kiaha* frame sticks,
  Over yonder in the mesquite.

QUAIL SONG [172]

The gray quails were bunched together,
  Coyote ran to look upon them.
The blue quails were bunched together;
  Coyote looked sidewise at them.

COYOTE SONG [172]

Coyote commences singing;
  Coyote commences singing.
The young woman hurries forth
  To hear the Coyote songs.

A hat of eagle feathers;
  A hat of eagle feathers,
A headdress was made for me
  That made my heart grow stronger.

The poetry of the North American Indians is especially rich, as might be expected, in songs to accompany the war-dance and in chants glorifying the warpath or requesting protection of the warriors. Good examples are to be found in the Southwest as well as in most other culture areas.

The following ritual is chanted by the Navahos at the time of going to battle.

PROTECTION SONG [144]

Now, Slayer of the Alien Gods, among men am I.
Now among the alien gods with weapons of magic am I.

Rubbed with the summits of the mountains,
Now among the alien gods with weapons of magic am I.
Now upon the beautiful trail of old age
Now among the alien gods with weapons of magic am I.

Now, Offspring of the Water, among men am I.
Now among the alien gods with weapons of magic am I.
Rubbed with the water of the summits,
Now among the alien gods with weapons of magic am I.
Now upon the beautiful trail of old age,
Now among the alien gods with weapons of magic am I.

Now, Lightning of the Thunder, among men am I.
Now among the alien gods with weapons of magic am I.
Rubbed with the summit of the sky,
Now among the alien gods with weapons of magic am I.
Now upon the beautiful trail of old age,
Now among the alien gods with weapons of magic am I.

Now, Altsodoniglehi, among men am I.
Now among the alien gods with weapons of magic am I.
Rubbed with the summits of the earth,
Now among the alien gods with weapons of magic am I.
Now upon the beautiful trail of old age,
Now among the alien gods with weapons of magic am I.

An ancient Navaho war-chant from another translator was supposed to have been made by the god Nayenezrani, and tells how this war-god hurls his enemies into the ground, one after another, with the weapon of the lightning. "The four lightnings strike from him in all directions, and return, for lightning always looks as if it flashed out and then went back."

WAR-SONG [44]

Lo, the flint youth, he am I.
The flint youth.

Nayenezrani, lo, behold me, he am I,
Lo, the flint youth, he am I,
The flint youth.

Moccasins of black flint have I;
    Lo, the flint youth, he am I,
       The flint youth.

Leggings of black flint have I;
    Lo, the flint youth, he am I,
       The flint youth.

Tunic of black flint have I;
    Lo, the flint youth, he am I,
       The flint youth.

Bonnet of black flint have I;
    Lo, the flint youth, he am I,
       The flint youth.

Clearest, purest flint the heart
Living strong within me—heart of flint;
    Lo, the flint youth, he am I,
       The flint youth.

Now the zigzag lightnings four
    From me flash,
Striking and returning,
    From me flash;
    Lo, the flint youth, he am I,
       The flint youth.

There where'er the lightnings strike,
Into the ground they hurl the foe—
Ancient folk with evil charms,
One upon another, dashed to earth;
    Lo, the flint youth, he am I,
       The flint youth.

Living evermore,
Feared of all forevermore,
    Lo, the flint youth, he am I,
       The flint youth.

Lo, the flint youth, he am I,
    The flint youth.

The following scalp-dance comes from the pueblo of Santa Clara, whose people sometimes warred with the followers of Flint Youth. The Coyote gets his ceremonial name of Stretched-Out-in-Dew to suggest his activities lying in wait to devour slain warriors.

SCALP-DANCE SONG [186]

Next after comes Coyote, Stretched-Out-in-Dew,
Next after braves of yesterday or the day before!
To Blue Earth town of the Navahos we go
And arriving we shall kill. So that is why
Coyote, Stretched-Out-in-Dew, sits straight and ready.
Wi-ya-he-na, a-nde-a-a. The next scalp!

Navaho youths! your fault alone it is
That now you die fallen along your house.
Your fault alone it is that now you die,
Fallen along your house with earth-streaked thighs,
That now your mouths are stopped and streaked with earth.
Ho-o-wi-na, a-ye-a-a. The next scalp!

Short shrift was given the Pueblo brave who died on the field of battle. If possible, a secret grave was made for him; he was placated with a gift of food, and almost summarily dismissed from mind.

DEAD ON THE WARPATH [186]

This very day, a little while ago, you lived
But now you are neither man nor woman;
Breathless you are, for the Navahos killed you!
Then remember us not, for here and now
We bring you your food. Then take and keep
Your earth-walled place: once! twice!
Three times! four times! Then leave us now!

A brief war song of the Pimas is given by Russell:

SCALP SONG [172]

There arose in the East Land
One whom I met there smoking
Flowerlike cigarettes.

Running dazed and falsely speaking
  Pitiable and faint-hearted
I feel at Crooked Mountain.

There I'm going, there I'm going.
  I have to drink the liquor
That makes me stagger as I run.

Vulture arose from Sandy Hill
  Shining upon the land around.

This song was accompanied by a dance. An even briefer war song
is given by the same translator:

PIMA WAR SONG [172]

Over that black sandy land,
  Over the top came running,
Over the top came running.
  The Apache slave was killed
And his hide tanned for leather.

Few lyrical love songs or love charms have been collected in the
Southwest. Spinden, however, has translated a few from the Tewa,
of which the following modern song, designed to encourage a lover,
is a good example:

SHADOWS [186]

That somebody, my own special one,
Even his shadow and his voice are loved.
His footfall even! But what can I do?
That other one, oh how I hate his shadow!
His shirt is fine and white, his hat is gray,
His leggings and his shoes are beaded bright,
His neckerchief is gay and yellow—but
For all his clothes, his face, his face is black!

The most common children's songs among the Indians are the
cradle-songs chanted or hummed by the squaws. Many of these
songs have no words, or only nonsense words. A few, however, are
worth remembering. Here is a cradle-song from the Hopi tribe. *Puva*
means "sleep."

HOPI LULLABY [44]

Puva, puva, puva,
In the trail the beetles
On each other's backs are sleeping,
So on mine, my baby, thou.
Puva, puva, puva!

This is a "stop-crying song for naughty children" which is supposed to be sung by the Owl *Katzina:*

HOPI OWL SONG [44]

Owls, Owls, big owls and little,
Staring, glaring, eyeing each other;
Children, from your cradle-boards, oh see!
Now the owls are looking at you, looking at you;
Saying, "Any crying child, Yellow-Eyes will eat him up."
Saying, "Any naughty child, Yellow-Eyes will eat him up."

Another amusing lullaby comes from the Tewa pueblos, where the children are threatened with the masked giant creatures who come to the village with whips to punish bad boys and girls.

LULLABY OF THE CANNIBAL GIANTS [186]

Stop crying! Go to sleep, my little boy Primrose.
That Saveyo Sendo will take you if you cry.
Over there he will eat you, if you do not stop crying;
Right now he will eat you, if you do not stop crying.
That Saveyo Sendo in his bag he will put you.
Stop crying! Go to sleep, my little boy Primrose.
Over there he will take you, then I will be crying!
Very thick now are the leaves of the cottonwood,
Very thick now are the leaves of the willow,
There he will take you in under the willow,
That Saveyo Sendo whose teeth we all fear.
Over there now, if you do not stop crying,
Over there now, on the crest of the mountains,
Those Saveyo walk and they hear every sound.
And there in the mountains that one he will take you,
Where now they are taking the big boys and girls.

Game songs are widely found in the Southwest. The following song translated by Matthews has been reprinted several times.

MAGPIE SONG [142]

The magpie! The magpie! Here underneath
In the white of his wings are the footsteps of morning.
It dawns! It dawns!

Some readers might be surprised to discover that it is a Navaho gambling song, uttered by a player at one stage of the complicated moccasin game. The lovely comparison of the white-margined wings of the bird with the paling edges of false dawn would seem to lift these lines above the commonplace ejaculations usually heard during a gambling game.

The game, as Matthews explains, employs eight half-buried moccasins in which a pebble is concealed, and the two sides take turns in guessing the hiding place. It is often played for high stakes, and is played only at night, because the pebble cannot be successfully hidden in daylight. The Navahos have a superstition, however, that anyone who plays when the sun is shining will be struck blind. "I have heard," the translator says, "that on some occasions, when the stakes are heavy and the day begins to dawn on an undecided contest, they close all the apertures of the lodge with blankets, blacken the skin around their eyes, place a watch outside to prevent intrusion, and for a short time continue their sport." [142] It would be at the approach of such a time that the "Magpie Song" is chanted.

An elaborate myth is the background for all these songs of the moccasin game. One Indian who had made this sport "the study of his life" averred that there was nothing that walked or flew or crept or crawled that had not at least one appropriate song in the game. For instance, in the myth the god Yeitso was kept from guessing correctly because the gopher would secretly transfer the pebble to another moccasin. This is the origin of the following taunting verse:

GOPHER SONG [142]

Gopher sees where the stone is,
Gopher sees where the stone is.
Strike on! Strike on!

The player is urged to strike by tapping the chosen moccasin with a stick. Another animal song from the moccasin game will serve as a final example.

GROUND-SQUIRREL SONG [142]

The squirrel in his shirt stands up there,
The squirrel in his shirt stands up there;
Slender, he stands up there; striped, he stands up there.

From the Pima tribe comes a song which is sung on the evening before the day of a foot race:

FOOT RACE SONG [172]

Many people have gathered together,
 I am ready to start in the race,
And the Swallow with beating wings
 Cools me in readiness for the word.

Far in the west stands the black mountain
 Around which our racers ran at noon.
Who is this man running with me,
 The shadow of whose hands I see?

Some Indian tribes have songs which are chanted when the men and women foregather for social dancing and entertainment. Not many of these social dance songs have furnished lyrics for the collector. One example from the Pima tribe, to be sung at fiestas which were accompanied by dancing, can here be given:

SWALLOW SONG [172]

Now the Swallow begins its singing;
 Now the Swallow begins his singing.
And the women who are with me,
 The poor women commence to sing.

The Swallows met in the standing cliffs;
 The Swallows met in the standing cliffs.
And the rainbows arched above me,
 There the blue rainbow arches met.

⚞ 5 ⚟

HORSE NATIONS OF THE PLAINS

THE TRIBES in the sky-vaulted expanse between the Mississippi River and the Rocky Mountains represent several different language families with different histories of migration. As one would expect, there are also some differences in cultural habits; but a number of traits can be found in common which have developed from the needs of living in the immense prairie.

The central tier of tribes inhabiting the range between the Canadian border and the Texas Panhandle, including the Teton Sioux or Dakota, Arapaho, Cheyenne, Kiowa, and Comanche, show what is probably the typical culture. They followed the buffalo, and were meat eaters depending little on agriculture or fishing. They dressed in skins of the buffalo or deer, were expert in leather and rawhide work, used a circular shield, carried "medicine bundles," had many secret societies and a loose social organization usually needed only to hold together a small band, and performed the Sun Dance as a unifying ritual ceremony. The tepee was their movable dwelling as they followed the ranging buffalo, and in earlier days they used dogs to drag their possessions after them bundled on long poles—the well-known travois. On the eastern rim of the plains were other tribes which shared many of the central traits and in addition went in for some agriculture and often supplemented tepee life with the erection of huts covered with grass, bark, or earth, and substituted for the Sun Dance more elaborate ceremonies in honor of the Maize Mother, as well as shamanistic displays and feats of conjuring. Important among these tribes were the Mandan, Hidatsa, Omaha, Pawnee, Kansa, Osage, and Wichita.

The complete dependence of the Plains Indians upon the hordes of buffalo was well described by one of the friars with Coronado: "With the skins they make their houses, with the skins they clothe and shoe themselves, of the skins they make rope, and also of the wool; from the sinews they make thread, with which they sew their clothes and also their houses; from the bones they make awls; the dung serves them for wood, because there is nothing else in that country; the stomachs serve them for pitchers and vessels from which they drink; they live on the flesh."

After the coming of the white man, the horse was adopted and led to a revolutionary change in the ease with which life on the prairies could be supported. Most of the Plains tribes became "horse Indians" before the United States acquired the Louisiana Purchase; by that time a Plains Indian was rarely seen afoot. The horse, clumsy in the uncleared woodlands and useless in the deserts or high peaks, was perfectly suited to grassland existence. Mounted, the hunters could now pursue the buffalo on better than equal terms—especially when armed with another white-man gift, the gun—and often a band would range five hundred miles during a season. Unfortunately, when the Indians became expert cavalrymen, fighting and fleeing were also more easy and exciting, and raiding over great distances became the most popular way for a Plains tribe to increase its wealth; stealing horses was an ingrained pastime with them. Greater mobility led to an intensification of the nomadic habits of the mid-country native. The Indian that we usually think of as being most truly an Indian—the Indian of the movies and Wild West novel—is probably one of the Plains tribesmen, with a feathered war bonnet and moccasins of buffalo hide, galloping bareback on a painted mustang.

The Plains singers and chanters devised a number of extensive ritual ceremonials, and were also known for their hunting songs, curing spells, and war songs. An interesting mystical revival of the late nineteenth century, the so-called Ghost Dance Religion, manifested itself most strongly among the ritual-minded Plains tribes. The most important translators of poetry from this region are Alice C. Fletcher among the Pawnees, Francis La Flesche among the Osages, both Fletcher and La Flesche for the Omaha tribe, and James Mooney and Frances Densmore as collectors of Ghost Dance songs. Natalie Curtis has some songs from the Kiowa, George Grinnell from the Cheyenne, Miss Densmore from the Mandan and Hidatsa (whose songs are short, with few words), and "Stanley Vestal" from the Dakota of Sitting Bull's time. Several important tribes of this area, such as the Crow, Ute, Iowa, and Comanche, have not contributed much to the body of Indian poetry in translation.

Composing personal verses was encouraged by the fact that membership in many of the tribal secret societies depended upon experiencing some mystical vision, which was embodied in a song. These vision songs might be made in youth after vigil and fasting, or later in life through the inspiration of dream states. "Every Indian boy," writes Miss Densmore, "at the age of about twelve years, was expected to fast for several days and watch for the dream or 'vision' in which he saw his individual 'spirit helper,' and to receive 'spirit help,' he sang the song and also performed certain prescribed acts." [54] She cites as an example a personal medicine song composed when a young Sioux warrior had dreamed that he would be aided throughout life by the owl and the crow.

DREAM SONG [54]

> At night may I roam,
> Against the winds may I roam,
> At night may I roam,
> When the owl is hooting may I roam.
>
> At dawn may I roam,
> Against the winds may I roam,
> At dawn may I roam,
> When the crow is calling may I roam.

Warfare and bloodshed were the common experiences of most of the Plains tribes, and in the lengthy ceremonials of such groups as the Pawnees and Osages we find an intense expression of the need to reconcile the demands of war and peace, of lawless adventure and spiritual contemplation, of individualism in survival and traditionalism in nature-worship. This integration and harmony is found best in the rituals of the Pawnee tribe at the crossroads of the Plains, whose ideals often reach the dignity of philosophy. Perhaps it is not surprising that the Pawnee, whose hand was against every other tribe, was most apt in devising words and acts to represent spiritual calm and spiritual strength. The Hako ceremony of the Pawnee, a consecration of the children of the tribe to the protection of the symbolic eagle and corn plant, is also a prayer for peace in a group where war ever waited beyond the circle of the band's lodges.

The Hako (the word is taken from the Pawnee name for symbolic articles used in the ritual) is a very old dramatic ceremony which was not confined to the Pawnee tribe alone. It was ritualized to the last movement of the participants and to the exact traditional phraseology of the chants, and contained no less than ninety-five separate songs in the cycle and nine incidental songs which might be interpolated at any time. The actual ceremony, which followed an initial period of preparatory rites, occupied five days and nights, and involved a processional progress through the countryside from one camp to another. It was undertaken when one person wished to show unusual honor to a member of another tribe, or of another clan of his own tribe. The first person was called the Father, and the person to be honored was called the Son, leader of the group of Children. The purpose of the ceremony, according to Miss Fletcher, translator of many Hako songs, was twofold: "First, to benefit certain individuals by bringing to them the promise of children, long life, and plenty; second, to affect the social relations of those who took part in it, by establishing a bond between two distinct groups of persons, belonging to different clans, gentes, or tribes, which was to insure between them friendship and peace." [90]

There is a strong reliance in the Hako upon the old symbols for the male and female cosmic forces—day and night, sun and moon, heavens and earth; and symbolic objects are used as well. "The eagle and the ear of corn also represent in general the male and female forces, but each is specialized in a manner peculiar to these rites. There are two eagles; the white, representing the male, the father, the defender; and the brown, representing the female, the mother, the nestmaker. In the treatment of these eagles the dual forces are still further represented. The feathers of the white or male eagle are hung upon a stem painted green to symbolize the earth, the female principle; while those of the brown or female eagle are hung upon the stem painted blue to symbolize the heavens, the male principle. The same treatment of the corn is observed. The ear of corn, which is born of Mother Earth, is symbolically painted to represent a living contact with the heavens." [90]

Miss Fletcher undertook, as was mentioned in Chapter 1, to make not only a literal, but an interpretative and rhythmic translation of the Hako songs, in consultation with a well known leader of the ceremony among the Chaui band of Pawnees; and comment was made in that chapter upon the validity of her practice of supplying varied meanings for identical lines, based upon the symbolism of the accompanying ritual acts. A few of the more representative pieces of this lengthy ceremonial are given here. Others which might have been included have been omitted because of too frequent use of poeticized contractions and of rhetorical inversions—a stylistic failing of several otherwise capable translators. The following four rhythmic translations, then, have been here chosen from the Hako ceremony.

THE HAKO PARTY PRESENTED TO THE POWERS [90]
>   Look down, West gods, look upon us! We gaze
>   afar on your dwelling.
>   Look down while here we are standing, look
>   down upon us, ye mighty!
>   Ye thunder gods, now behold us!
>   Ye lightning gods, now behold us!
>   Ye that bring life, now behold us!
>   Ye that bring death, now behold us!

Look down, South gods, look upon us! We gaze
    afar on your dwelling.
Look down while here we are standing, look
    down upon us, ye mighty!
Ye daylight gods, now behold us!
Ye sunshine gods, now behold us!
Ye increase gods, now behold us!
Ye plenty gods, now behold us!

Look down, North gods, look upon us! We gaze
    afar on your dwelling.
Look down while here we are standing, look
    down upon us, ye mighty!
Ye darkness gods, now behold us!
Ye moonlight gods, now behold us!
Ye that direct, now behold us!
Ye that discern, now behold us!

DAYLIGHT [90]

Day is here! Day is here, is here!
Arise, my son, lift thine eyes. Day is here! Day is here, is here!
Day is here! Day is here, is here!
Look up, my son, and see the day. Day is here! Day is here, is here!
Day is here! Day is here, is here!

Lo, the deer! Lo, the deer, the deer
Comes from her covert of the night! Day is here! Day is here, is here!
Lo, the deer! Lo, the deer, the deer!
All creatures wake and see the light. Day is here! Day is here, is here!
Day is here! Day is here, is here!

THE SIXTEEN CIRCUITS OF THE LODGE—THIRD SONG [90]

O'er the prairie flits in ever widening circles the shadow of a bird
    about me as I walk;
Upward turn my eyes, Kawas looks upon me, she turns with flapping
    wings and far away she flies.

Round about a tree in ever widening circles an eagle flies, alertly
    watching o'er his nest;
Loudly whistles he, a challenge sending afar, o'er the country wide it
    echoes, there defying foes.

The Pawnees deified the stars, and many of their myths tell of the gods Morning Star and Evening Star. Their villages were governed by star shrines where the powers of heaven were invoked. Their sages were also practical astronomers who computed the important dates for corn-planting and other calendar events. This is an invocation to the Pleiades, from the Hako ceremony:

SONG TO THE PLEIADES [90]

Look as they rise, rise
Over the line where sky meets the earth;
Pleiades!
Lo! They ascending, come to guide us,
Leading us safely, keeping us one;
Pleiades,
Teach us to be, like you, united.

Miss Fletcher has also translated some of the exalted and moving rituals of the Omaha tribe. In particular, this invocation to the gods of nature to protect an infant member of the group is worthy of remembrance:

INTRODUCTION OF THE CHILD TO THE COSMOS [95]

Ho! Ye Sun, Moon, Stars, all ye that move in the heavens,
    I bid you hear me!
Into your midst has come a new life.
    Consent ye, I implore!
Make its path smooth, that it may reach the brow of the first hill!

Ho! Ye Winds, Clouds, Rain, Mist, all ye that move in the air,
    I bid you hear me!
Into your midst has come a new life.
    Consent ye, I implore!
Make its path smooth, that it may reach the brow of the second hill!

Ho! Ye Hills, Valleys, Rivers, Lakes, Trees, Grasses, all ye of the
    earth,
    I bid you hear me!
Into your midst has come a new life.
    Consent ye, I implore!
Make its path smooth, that it may reach the brow of the third hill!

Ho! Ye Birds, great and small, that fly in the air,
Ho! Ye Animals, great and small, that dwell in the forest,
Ho! Ye Insects that creep among the grasses and burrow in the
    ground—
    I bid you hear me!
Into your midst has come a new life.
    Consent ye, I implore!
Make its path smooth, that it may reach the brow of the fourth hill!

Ho! All ye of the heavens, all ye of the air, all ye of the earth;
    I bid you all to hear me!
Into your midst has come a new life.
    Consent ye, consent ye all, I implore!
Make its path smooth—then shall it travel beyond the four hills!

No less than five large volumes of rituals from the Osage tribe have been translated by Dr. Francis La Flesche. The following is a typical Osage chant. It is a part of the "Child-Naming Rite," and the thought is found in many forms in the work of La Flesche and earlier in that of J. Owen Dorsey. The tale runs that when the People of the Seven Fireplaces went to the "Stainless Bird" (in another version, the eagle) and said to him: "The little ones have nothing of which to make their bodies"—meaning that they had no symbol for the long life which they craved—he replied in the wise and dignified words given below.

OLD-AGE CHANT [135c]

Verily, at that time and place, it has been said, in this house,
The Hónga, a people who possess seven fireplaces,
Spake to one another, saying: Lo, we have nothing of which to make
    our bodies.
Then, at that very time,
They spake to the bird that has no stains [evil disposition],
Saying: O, grandfather,
The little ones have nothing of which to make their bodies.
Then, at that very time,
The bird that has no stains
Spake, saying: When the little ones make of me their bodies,
They shall always live to see old age, as they travel the path of life.

Again the bird spake:
Behold my toes that are gathered together in folds,
Which I have made to be the sign of my old age.
When the little ones make of me the means of reaching old age,
They shall always live to see old age, as they travel the path of life.

Behold, also, the wrinkles upon my shins,
Which I have made to be the sign of my old age.
When the little ones make of me the means of reaching old age,
They shall always live to see old age, as they travel the path of life.

The bird that has no stain
Again spake, saying: Behold the wrinkles upon my knees,
Which I have made to be the sign of my old age.
When the little ones make of me the means of reaching old age,
They shall always live to see old age, as they travel the path of life.

Behold the muscles of my breast, gathered together as in a fold,
Which I have made to be the sign of my old age.
When the little ones make of me the means of reaching old age,
They shall always live to see old age, as they travel the path of life.

Behold the flaccid muscles of my arms,
Which I have made to be the sign of my old age.
When the little ones make of me the means of reaching old age,
They shall always live to see old age, as they travel the path of life.

Behold the bend of my shoulders,
Which I have made to be the sign of my old age.
When the little ones make of me the means of reaching old age,
They shall always live to see their shoulders bent with age, as they
    travel the path of life.

Behold the flaccid muscles of my throat,
Which I have made to be the sign of my old age.
When the little ones make of me the means of reaching old age,
They shall always live to see old age, as they travel the path of life.

Behold the folds in the corners of my eyelids,
Which I have made to be the signs of my old age.
When the little ones make of me the means of reaching old age,
They shall always live to see the corners of their eyelids folded with
    age, as they travel the path of life.

Behold my eyelids that are gathered into folds,
Which I have made to be the signs of my old age.
When the little ones make of me the means of reaching old age,
They shall always live to see their eyelids gathered into folds with
    age, as they travel the path of life.

Behold the hair on the crown of my head, now grown thin,
Which I have made to be the sign of my old age.
When the little ones make of me the means of reaching old age,
They shall always live to see the hair on the crown of their heads
    grow thin with age, as they travel the path of life.

Another passage from the Osage rites is of considerable symbolic
significance:

CHILD-NAMING RITE OF THE BOW PEOPLE [135c]

I am a person who is fitted for use as a symbol.
Verily, in the midst of the rushing waters
Abides my being.
Verily, I am a person who has made of the waters his body.

Behold the right side of the river,
Of which I have made the right side of my body.
When the little ones make of me their bodies
And use the right side of the river
To make their bodies,
The right side of their bodies shall be free from all causes of death.

Behold the left side of the river,
Of which I have made the left side of my body.
When the little ones also make of it the left side of their bodies,
The left side of their bodies shall always be free from all causes of
    death.

Behold the channel of the river,
Of which I have made the hollow of my body.
When the little ones make of me their bodies,
The hollow of their bodies shall always be free from all causes of
    death.

The expression "make of me their bodies" means, as in the previous
ritual, "make of me an ideal for the formation of character." This

is part of a ceremonial by which the child is brought into touch with
the ever-flowing waters, the red cedar (an everlasting tree), and the
life-giving corn—symbols to guide him in his future growth.

The Osage rituals include a group of "Black Bear" songs which
relate to the myth about how the soil of the earth was given to the
people by the black bear as a sign of vigil when they appealed to
the divine power for aid in overcoming their enemies. "This act
of the bear in disclosing the sacred soil is a sacred and mysterious
act, therefore he who is to open the earth in order to take from it
with his hands the soil to be used in his vigil must simulate in detail
the actions of the bear." [135b] The soil is used to blacken the face for
the later rites.

BLACK BEAR SONG [135b]

Sacred is the act by which my hands are browned,
It is the act by which I offer my prayer.

Sacred is the act by which my hands are blackened,
It is the act by which I offer my prayer.

Sacred is the act by which my face is browned,
It is the act by which I offer my prayer.

Sacred is the act by which my face is blackened,
It is the act by which I offer my prayer.

Sacred is the light of day that falls upon my face,
The day on which my prayers are finished.

La Flesche has translated a ritual prayer for buffalo hunting, also
from the "Rite of Vigil." These songs "relate to the buffalo, a food
animal, and to the corn, a food plant. Both of these forms of life are
held sacred because they are believed to be direct gifts to the people
from the Mysterious Power, whence comes life in all its multifarious
forms, the ability to move, to reproduce its kind, in order that each
one may bear its particular part in the great drama of life." [135b] The
song does not ask directly for luck in the chase; the rites merely
imply this, and the language is expressive of an appeal for divine aid.
The translator remarks that this song has been the source of personal
names taken from each stanza: He-Whose-Tread-Makes-the-Earth-

Rumble, Great-Thighs, Tail-Curved Back, Humped-Shoulder, Shakes-His-Mane, and Curved-Horns. The lines offer a succinct suggestion of the most important characteristics of the buffalo bull as he appeared to the Plains Indian.

THE RISING OF THE BUFFALO MEN [135b]

I rise, I rise,
I, whose tread makes the earth to rumble.

I rise, I rise,
I, in whose thighs there is strength.

I rise, I rise,
I, who whips his back with his tail when in rage.

I rise, I rise,
I, in whose humped shoulder there is power.

I rise, I rise,
I, who shakes his mane when angered.

I rise, I rise,
I, whose horns are sharp and curved.

Also from La Flesche comes this Osage planting song. It is not a work song, but is sung at the end of the rites of initiation in which women take part. "The woman is the planter, the cultivator, the harvester of the corn, and this little scene is meant to portray the important part she plays in the drama of life." Each line which follows is the first of a stanza, which is followed by four lines of repetitions or vocables.

PLANTING SONG [135a]

I have made a footprint, a sacred one.
I have made a footprint, through it the blades push upward.
I have made a footprint, through it the blades radiate.
I have made a footprint, over it the blades float in the wind.
I have made a footprint, over it the ears lean toward one another.
I have made a footprint, over it I bend the stalk to pluck the ears.
I have made a footprint, over it the blossoms lie gray.
I have made a footprint, smoke arises from my house.

I have made a footprint, there is cheer in my house.
I have made a footprint, I live in the light of day.

Curing songs were found among the Plains tribes. Representative is the following ritual recited by the Omaha shaman while the sweat-lodge was being prepared for treating the patient:

CURING RITUAL [95]

Ho! Aged One, *eçka* [I pray].
At a time when there were gathered together seven persons,
You sat in the seventh place, it is said,
And of the seven you alone possessed knowledge of all things, Aged
    One, *eçka*.
When in their longing for protection and guidance
The people sought in their minds for a way,
They beheld you sitting with assured permanency and endurance
In the center where converged the paths;
There, exposed to the violence of the four winds, you sat,
Possessed with power to receive supplications, Aged One, *eçka*.
Where is his mouth, by which there may be utterance of speech?
Where is his heart, to which there may come knowledge and under-
    standing?
Where are his feet, whereby he may move from place to place?
We question in wonder,
Yet verily it is said you alone have power to receive supplications,
    Aged One, *eçka*.
I have desired to go yet farther in the path of life with my little
    ones,
Without pain, without sickness,
Beyond the second, third, and fourth period of life's pathway, Aged
    One, *eçka*.
O hear! This is my prayer,
Although uttered in words poorly put together, Aged One, *eçka*.

Only a few love songs come from the prairies. A *wáuwaan* or "woman song" with a love story behind it is given by Miss Fletcher from the Omaha tribe. The explanation is as follows: "The stanza opens with her lament addressed to her lover, who, having won her

affection, has so possessed her thoughts that when he sang without
the tent and the family asked 'Who is it that sings?' the girl uncon-
sciously lets drop his name. All eyes are turned on her and then she
realizes what she has done."

WOMAN SONG [95]

Alas! I have made myself known, *the!*
Alas! I have made myself known, *the!*
Last night when you sang I uttered your name, *the!*
Alas! I have made myself known, *the! hi.*
"Who is it that sings?" *the!* they said, and I sitting there, *the!*
"Waguntha is passing," I said, *the!*
It was your name I uttered, *the! hi.*

The women of the fighting Plains braves were staunch in their
thoughts toward the men who had gone on the warpath, and this
spirit is embodied in a certain sort of love song called the "wind
song." Among the Kiowas, observes Natalie Curtis, "Gomda Daagya
(Wind-Songs) are war songs made while the men are on the war-
path, and are sung by those at home who think of the distant
warriors, or by the men on the warpath who think of their loved
ones at home. . . . So might the maiden sing, thinking of her lover;
so might the young warrior sing, thinking of the maid. Such songs
are called Wind-Songs because they are songs of loneliness and
longing like the open prairie where there is only the sweep of the
wind." Here is such a song made by a Kiowa girl:

WIND SONG [44]

Idlers and cowards are here at home now,
Whenever they wish, they see their beloved ones.
Oh, idlers and cowards are here at home now,
But the youth I love is gone to war, far hence.
Weary, lonely, for me he longs.

Another song of the Kiowas reveals the thoughts of the maiden
waiting for her first lover, and scorning the offers of horses which
another wooer has made to her father.

WARPATH SONG [44]

Ah, I never, never can forget
The playful word you spoke long since.
This man who seeks to marry me,
He with his sore-backed ponies,
    What's he to me!

A similar kind of song, sung by the Cheyenne scouts or "wolves," has been described by Grinnell. These "wolf songs" were sung when the men felt downhearted, lonely, or discouraged, and often referred to the singer's sweetheart. On the other hand, many of them had words addressed by the leader to his war followers, such as this example:

WOLF SONG [109]

Take courage;
Do not be frightened;
Follow where you see me riding my white horse.

Many good war songs, as might be expected, come from the Plains paladins. The famous Sitting Bull, of the Sioux or Dakota tribe, was a medicine man as well as a war chief, and a great part of his personal power may be ascribed to his skill in composing and chanting stirring songs. A number of these are given by "Stanley Vestal" in his biography of this warrior.

Early in his life, Sitting Bull became a friend of the birds, and, indeed, he ascribed the saving of his life to a dream in which an encounter with a grizzly bear was foretold by a bird. After escaping by feigning death beneath the paws of the bear, the young man addressed this song to the friendly yellow-hammer:

SITTING BULL'S SONG [203]

Pretty bird, you saw me and took pity on me;
You wished me to survive among the people.
O Bird People, from this day always you shall be my relatives!

During his life Sitting Bull had many occasions to risk death in battle, and to lead his men with stirring chants such as this:

YOUNG MEN, HELP ME [203]

Young men, help me, do help me!
I love my country so;
That is why I am fighting.

This, his favorite war song, suggests that his valor has doomed him
to an instant death on the field:

BATTLE SONG [203]

No chance for me to live;
Mother, you might as well mourn.

It is told how Sitting Bull once heard a wolf singing his lonely
fierce chant. He listened, and found that the wolf's advice was
addressed to him and was good. This is the song he afterward made:

SONG OF THE WOLF [203]

I am a lonely wolf, wandering pretty nearly all over the world.
　He, he, he!
What is the matter? I am having a hard time, friend.
This that I tell you, you will have to do also.
Whatever I want, I always get it.
Your name will be big, as mine is big. *Hiu! Hiu!*

A Pawnee war song given by Brinton has a reflective turn. "It is
one which is sung when a warrior undertakes to perform some
particularly daring individual exploit, which may well cost him his
life. The words seem to call upon the gods to decide whether this
mortal life is only an illusion, or a divine truth under the guidance
of divine intelligence."

LET US SEE [26]

Let us see, is this real,
Let us see, is this real,
Let us see, is this real,
This life I am living?
Ye gods, who dwell everywhere,
Let us see, is this real,
This life I am living?

A large volume of war and peace ceremonials from the Osage tribe
has been translated by La Flesche. One of these prefigures the hard-
ships to be met by the young warriors, of which the greatest on the
march is thirst.

DRY IS MY TONGUE [136]

> Dry is my tongue from marching,
> **O,** my elder brother, **O,** my elder brother.
> Dry is my tongue from marching,
> And, lo, death draws near to me.
> Dry is my tongue from marching,
> **O,** my elder brother, **O,** my elder brother.
> Dry is my tongue from marching.

The following Osage song, to celebrate the taking of scalps on
the warpath, is not a personal exultation. It is chanted by the leader
and the words are "uttered, as it were, by the symbolic man who
represents the unity of the people. . . . The words are not intended
as a boast but as a declaration that the will and the determination of
the people to defend and to maintain their life as an organized body
has now been put into execution." The song, then, is not a ballad
to commemorate a particular battle; the words are always exactly
the same.

SONG OF THE KILLING [136]

O ho, it is I who served them thus,
I who brought these deeds to pass,
A he the, a he the the.
O ho, it is I who fell upon them unawares,
I who brought these deeds to pass,
A he the, a he the the.

O ho, it is I who lay them low, etc.
O ho, it is I who lay them reddened on the earth, etc.
O ho, it is I who lay their bones to bleach on the earth, etc.
O ho, it is I who lay them yellowing on the earth, etc.
O ho, it is I who lay them darkening on the earth, etc.
O ho, it is I who snatch from them their remaining days, etc.

On the return of the war party, the chief of the victorious Osages led them in this song, suiting the actions to the words:

SONG OF ENTERING THE VILLAGE [136]

I am home, I am home, I am home,
I have now come to the land that is home.
I have now come to the border of the village.
I have now come to the foot-worn soil of the village.
I have now come to the rear of the sacred house.
I have now come to the end of the sacred house.
I have now come to the door of the sacred house.
I have now come inside of the sacred house.
I have now come to the kettle pole of the sacred house.
I have now come to the fireplace of the sacred house.
I have now come to the middle of the sacred house.
I have now come to the smoke vent of the sacred house.
I have now come into the midst of the light of day.

An appealing peace ritual, given by La Flesche in the same volume, which is too long for inclusion here, has an idea which should be mentioned. The form of this "Sky Ritual" is based upon the Osage "sky-controlling songs," which are incantations to assure good hunting weather. This rather mundane purpose has been made transcendent by the metaphorical vision of the ancient composer of the peace rite. As La Flesche says: "The sky mentioned in the ritual . . . is not the material sky that surrounds us, but the sky of conduct of men toward one another, a sky which might be overcast with dangerous and destructive clouds of war, but which could be influenced by men, through self-restraint, self-denial, and good will, which alone can avert the storms of hatred and malice, and make the sky of conduct clear and serene." [136] Such a ritual image could be made the basis for a firm and lasting peace.

A few game songs have been collected in the plains. Here are several songs from the Cheyenne hand-game, which centered about guessing which of the opponent's fists held the concealed "ball."

HAND-GAME SONG [55]

My ball is going around three times.
They are playing over there [in the spirit land].

The next song of this game, says Miss Densmore, was a "space-filling song," which was not sung either during the hiding or the dancing that form part of the play. "There is a resemblance," she adds, "between their words and those of the Ghost Dance with its strange visions."

THE RAVEN SAYS [55]

Our father above, I have seen.
The raven says, "There is going to be another judgment day."

SONGS OF THE GHOST DANCE RELIGION

The most important source of vision-inspired songs is the Ghost Dance Religion, a revivalist Indian cult which swept through the Plains Indians around 1890. This curious messianic religion was inspired by a Paiute medicine man named Wovoka, son of another prophet whose doctrines had aroused a wave of revivalism in northern California about 1870. The younger man about 1887 suffered a dangerous fever during an eclipse of the sun. He "died," and in a vision, wrote James Mooney, the main authority on the Ghost Dance, "was taken up into the other world. Here he saw God with all the people who had long ago died engaged in their old time sports and occupations, all happy and forever young. It was a pleasant land and full of game. . . . God told him he must go back and tell his people they must be good and love one another, have no quarreling and live in peace with the whites; that they must work, and not lie and steal; that they must put away the old practices that savored of war; that if they faithfully obeyed his instructions they would at last be reunited with their friends in the other world, where there would be no more death or sickness or old age. He was then given the dance which he was commanded to bring back to his people. By performing this dance at intervals, for five successive days each time, they would secure this happiness to themselves and hasten the event. . . . He then returned to earth, and he began to preach as he was directed, convincing the people by exercising the wonderful powers that he had given him." [149]

The preachments of Wovoka spread like wildfire from Nevada to the north and south, and especially to the east, across the plains. A number of Plains tribes who heard of the newest Indian messiah sent emissaries to hear his story. First the Arapahos and Shoshones of Wind River, and then the northern Cheyennes and the branches of the Sioux or Dakotas (Sitting Bull—not the Sioux chief, but an Arapaho holy man—was the chief proponent of the new belief among them) heard the message. In the fall of 1890, Sitting Bull came to Oklahoma to instruct the tribes there in the dance ceremony, and by putting many dancers into hypnotic trances during which they saw visions and created songs about their experiences, convinced the southern Plains tribes that they should welcome this spiritual movement. Shortly thereafter the Caddos, Wichitas, Kiowas, and Comanches began dancing; a year later the religion had come to the Iowas, Kansas, and Pawnees.

This gospel of resignationism, tinged with scraps of Christian ideas and a turning backward toward the lost, happy ways of the past, came to the Plains Indians at a moment when such a preachment found fertile soil. At this time, most of the buffalo herds, the main dependence of the plainsmen, had been slaughtered by the millions by white hide-hunters. The roving warriors were defeated and cooped up on reservations and told to till the soil like women, and in idleness lost the old stimuli of action, cultural creativeness, and spiritual unification through symbolic ritual. The Plains tribes, knowing that the future had little in store for them but decay and disease, at first found new hope in the doctrine of a happy future in the land of spirits or ghosts, but the frenzy soon was rigorously suppressed by the government and many adherents lapsed into apathy. Although the message of Wovoka was one of peace, the western Sioux, still warlike, used it as an incitement against the whites. Nervous misunderstanding of the meaning of these dances, in which numbers of Sioux in painted ghost-shirts took part, precipitated the massacre of Wounded Knee in the last days of 1890, during which American forces with Hotchkiss guns wiped out two hundred men, women and children in a few bloody moments. Thereafter the doctrine died out except as a furtive accompaniment of social dances and games.

The most interesting part of the Ghost Dance movement is perhaps the singing of songs which were composed during the trances of the worshipers. Hypnosis presumably induced the vision state, but it is possible that it was also caused by the eating of peyote, a drug which formed the basis of another Plains cult at about the same period. Peyote, the narcotic bud of a certain cactus, induces bright, quickly shifting images which rapidly merge into new images. A number of the Ghost Dance songs, as will be seen, refer to one object "turning into" another.

Concerning these songs, Mooney says: "The Ghost Dance songs are of the utmost importance in connection with the study of the messiah religion, as we find embodied in them much of the doctrine itself, with more of the special tribal mythologies, together with such innumerable references to old-time customs, ceremonies, and modes of life long since obsolete as make up a regular symposium of aboriginal thought and practice. There is no limit to the number of these songs, as every trance at every dance produces a new one, the trance subject after regaining consciousness embodying his experience in the spirit world in the form of a song, which is sung at the next dance and succeeding performances until superseded by other songs originating in the same way. Thus, a single dance may easily result in twenty or thirty new songs." [149]

The verse pattern for these songs is quite similar from tribe to tribe, and is stiff and fixed in form, consisting usually of two or three lines, each repeated once. It may be considered strange that so free and wild an experience as a trance vision should always be expressed in rigid poetic style. Possibly this verse form was adapted from the songs that were interpolated in the old gambling hand-games. A typical example of a Ghost Dance song is one from the early stage of the movement, a song from the Paiutes of Nevada, Wovoka's homeplace. In these few lines the doctrine of the "new earth" is apparently portrayed as coming white with snow, driven by a whirlwind.

THE WHIRLWIND [149]

The whirlwind! The whirlwind!
The snowy earth comes gliding,
The snowy earth comes gliding.

The largest number of Ghost Dance songs that have been collected come from the Arapaho tribe. Here is a song which relates the adventures of a man who in his vision found himself in a camp in the spirit world and was taken around by his father to meet other departed friends. "While they were going about," remarks Mooney, "a change came o'er the spirit of his dream, as so often happens in this fevered mental condition, and instead of his father he found a moose standing by his side."

MY FATHER, MY FATHER [149]

My father, my father,
While he was taking me around,
While he was taking me around,
He turned into a moose,
He turned into a moose.

A similar song, given below, is ascribed to Sitting Bull, who lost his life when being arrested as an inciter of the dance frenzy. The expression "You are the child of a crow" is interpreted by Mooney to refer to the singer's sacred character as an apostle of the dance; the crow was regarded as a messenger from the spirit world.

MY FATHER DID NOT RECOGNIZE ME [149]

My father did not recognize me [at first],
My father did not recognize me.
When again he saw me,
When again he saw me,
He said, "You are the offspring of a crow,"
He said, "You are the offspring of a crow."

Closely resembling these is a third Arapaho song:

MY FATHER, I AM LOOKING [149]

My father, my father—
I am looking at him,
I am looking at him.
He is beginning to turn into a bird,
He is beginning to turn into a bird.

In another song the dreamer says that the predicted spiritual new earth is about to come and blot out the old.

MY CHILDREN [149]

My children, my children,
Look! the earth is about to move,
Look! the earth is about to move.
My father tells me so,
My father tells me so.

The idea is repeated in a song from the Cheyenne tribe, in which the new earth is supposed to make a humming noise on its approach.

OUR FATHER HAS COME [149]

Our father has come,
Our father has come,
The earth has come,
The earth has come,
It is rising—*Eyé ye!*
It is rising—*Eyé ye!*
It is humming—*Ahé e ye!*
It is humming—*Ahé e ye!*

Another Cheyenne song pictures the movement of the mountains of the earth:

THE MOUNTAIN [149]

The mountain,
The mountain,
It is circling around,
It is circling around.
A hiya e yee heyé!
A hiya e yee heyé!

Similar songs are to be found among such far-flung tribes as the Paiute, the Comanche, the Caddo, the Kiowa, and the Sioux.

Some of the verses recorded among the Sioux are the most interesting both in imagery and in form. The following is, according to Mooney, another example of the songs where the spirit friend suddenly assumes the shape of a bird, a moose, or some other animal.

IT IS YOUR FATHER [149]

It is your father coming,
It is your father coming.
A spotted eagle is coming for you,
A spotted eagle is coming for you.

One of the best of the Sioux songs "summarized the whole hope of the Ghost Dance—the return of the buffalo and the departed dead, the message being brought to the people by the sacred birds, the eagle and the crow."

THE WHOLE WORLD IS COMING [149]

The whole world is coming.
A nation is coming, a nation is coming,
The Eagle has brought the message to the tribe.
The father says so, the father says so.
Over the whole earth they are coming.
The buffalo are coming, the buffalo are coming,
The Crow has brought the message to the tribe,
The father says so, the father says so.

In their confusion of Indian and Christian ideas, the revivalist singers sometimes used the word "Jesus" to refer to the recrudescent native messiah whose return was prophesied in the songs. This vision song was recorded among the Kiowa tribe.

GOD HAS HAD PITY ON US [149]

God has had pity on us,
God has had pity on us.
Jesus has taken pity on us,
Jesus has taken pity on us.
He teaches me a song,
He teaches me a song.
My song is a good one,
My song is a good one.

That all these features of the Ghost Dance singing are not the product of this one translator's style may be seen by comparing the Mooney versions with two songs from an Arapaho ceremony recorded by Miss Densmore.

IT WAS THE TURTLE [55]

A long time ago, when they were living;
A long time ago,
I guess it was the turtle.
That is what my father says;
That is what my father says.

The reference to the turtle is not explained; it is probably the report of a sacred vision figure.

HE, MY CHILDREN [55]

He, my children, here is another pipe.
Now I am going to holler on this earth.
Everything is in motion.

Another collector, Natalie Curtis, found this Ghost Dance song among the Teton Sioux; it is typical in form and content.

SONG OF THE SPIRIT-DANCE [44]

Thus the Father saith,
Lo, he now commandeth
All on earth to sing,
    To sing now.
Thus he hath spoken,
Thus he hath spoken.
Tell afar his message,
Tell afar his message!

⧬ 6 ⧬

HUNTERS OF THE EASTERN WOODLANDS

SCORES OF TRIBES in olden times ranged the eastern forests of the continent between the Mississippi River and the Atlantic Ocean, Hudson's Bay and the Gulf of Mexico. A tangle of language families and various legends of migration reveal that these tribes had many earlier origins. Most of these proud tribes that greeted the English colonists in the seventeenth century have disappeared from the scene, and their poetry died with them. Many others, as the white man invaded their hunting grounds, were forced westward and cribbed in the narrow confines of reservations. When we consider the decay of these once powerful tribes, it is surprising that any of their songs have survived; we are fortunate that a few important remnants of their olden rituals have come down to us.

The culture of this large but fairly homogeneous area may be subdivided into three belts corresponding to the main zones of environment.

Above the Great Lakes, the northern Chippewa (Ojibway), the woods Cree, and the Naskapi had a rather simple culture based on caribou hunting, the snaring of game, fishing, the birch-bark canoe, the conical skin- or bark-covered shelter, and the use of wooden utensils.

The middle body consisted of the central Algonkin (such as the Chippewa, Ottawa, Menominee, Sauk and Fox, Illinois, and Shawnee tribes) and the eastern Algonkin (Abenaki, Micmac, Passamaquoddy, and Delaware or Lenape tribes), separated by the wedge of intruding Iroquoian tribes (Huron or Wyandot, Erie, Susquehanna, and the "Six Nations"). The Iroquoian culture suggests a southern origin, and the predominant type is probably that of the large Chippewa group. Their characteristics were the casual cultivation of corn, squash, and beans; eating of fish, wild rice, maple sugar, and deer, bear, and buffalo meat; use of wood and bark vessels; sheltering in dome-shaped bark lodges in winter and rectangular bark houses in summer; making of dugouts and bark canoes; use of snowshoes; making of pack lines and fish nets; wearing of skin clothing and robes, some of which were woven of rabbit skin; bows, clubs, and tomahawks as weapons; taking of fish with hooks, spears, and nets; trapping and snaring of small game; and making of mats of reeds and cedar bark. Society was organized around the gens, or group descended in the male line; there were no social classes or formal property holders. Rituals included the scalp-dance and a secret initiation ceremony called the Midéwiwin; use of ceremonial bundles; many shamanistic performances and special formulas for treating the sick by roots and herbs; and the elaboration of songs for many uses in daily life. The Iroquoian tribes were good farmers and potters; they built fortifications around their villages or "castles" and lived in a unique "long house"; they made some use of the blowgun; they carved elaborate masks of wood to wear at the dances of their secret societies, and had a corn harvest festival. Their highly advanced political organization, the "League," made methodical conquests.

The southeastern area, whose ancient center of culture lay among the Natchez tribe of the lower Mississippi, had the Muskhogean (including the Choctaws and the Creeks) and lower Iroquoian families (Cherokees and Tuscaroras) as the chief groups. The following are the most distinctive southern traits: intensive agriculture and use of vegetable foods; raising of corn, pumpkins, melons, and tobacco, and quick adoption of European fruits and vegetables, as well as chickens, hogs, and cattle; hunting of deer, bear, and buffalo in western parts; fishing, and hunting of smaller game such as the turkey; rectangular houses with curved roofs, covered with thatch or bark; fortification of towns with palisades; use of dugout canoes; deerskin clothing; fine mats of cane and baskets of cane and splints; knives and darts of cane and blowguns as weapons; good pottery; some stone work; ceremonial houses or temples built upon mounds for sun worship, in which burned perpetual fires; a ritual ball game like lacrosse; elaborate planting and harvest rituals, especially the "busk" or fasting period, the kindling of the "new fire," and the ceremonial drinking of the purifying "black drink." They had a clan system and a group of chiefs (under the sacred influence of the Sun God) and four classes of subjects. Strong confederacies were often developed, such as that among the Creek towns. The medicine man held a prominent place in tribal councils.

The study of Indian poetry began among the tribes in the Eastern area, when Schoolcraft went to live among the Chippewas of the Lakes region. Besides Schoolcraft, Frances Densmore and Walter James Hoffman have translated Chippewa verse. Horatio Hale and Harriet M. Converse have given us ritual verse from the Iroquois, Daniel G. Brinton from the Lenape or Delaware tribe, John Reade from the Wabanaki, and J. Walker Fewkes from the Passamaquoddy. To the south, James Mooney has translated two volumes of Cherokee charms from Indian manuscripts, Miss Densmore has collected Choctaw songs, and John R. Swanton and Frank G. Speck have given us poetry from the Creek nations. Prominent in this region are fragments of verse that approach the narrative chronicle, such as the "Walam Olum"; unifying rituals such as the Iroquois confederacy rite of the Condoling Council; curing incantations; a number of love songs and love charms; war songs; and a few children's songs and social dance songs.

The Algonkin family, whose god was Manitou and whose culture hero was Manibozho with his Thunderbird messenger, were unique among the families of the continent in their use of picture writing on birch bark. The lives of these woodland people are suggested by the many words they gave to the American language in colonial times; a few of these Algonkin words are wigwam, tomahawk, wampum, toboggan, tump (line), moccasin, powwow, totem, squaw, papoose, sachem, sagamore, tamarack, hickory, pecan, persimmon, hominy, samp, succotash, pemmican, squash, caribou, wapiti, moose, opossum, raccoon, skunk, chipmunk, quahaug, muskellunge, menhadin, porgy, and terrapin.

One of the most admirable Algonkin tribes was the Delaware, who called themselves the Lenape. They held broad lands in the valley of the Delaware River, made many treaties with the invading white men, and in their heyday in colonial times were guided by a sage named Tamenend, a wise chief who appears in Cooper's *The Last of the Mohicans* and whose name, in the form "Tammany," was given to a New York political club that still flourishes. After the day of Tamenend, they succumbed to the pressure of white men from the east and the fierce Iroquois to the north and west, who about 1720 subjected them and won tribute. In despair, this once haughty tribe, the only northern group whose history has been recorded in a form approaching the chronicle, began to drift westward, and again and again sought peace, only to be forced further toward the setting sun, until when they finally settled in Oklahoma and Ontario, they had been reduced to a sixth of their former numbers and owned little more than a heap of broken treaties and a gloomy cynicism about white promises.

No record survives from the American Indians of any epic poem comparable to those of the European and Central Asiatic races. The most important translation which bears any resemblance to the epic form is the "Walam Olum" or "Red Score" of the Lenape tribe. Obviously a traditional rendering of their tribal history, this chronicle is a metrical recitative based upon picture-writing engraved on wood; these little drawings present a narrative with striking economy of depiction, and can be interpreted, with a little puzzling, by one familiar with conventional Indian symbols. Brinton, the translator of the lines that went with these mnemonic pictures, explains the provenance and value of the "Walam Olum" thus: "It is a genuine native production, which was repeated orally to someone indifferently conversant with the Delaware language, who wrote it down to the best of his ability. In its present form it can, as a whole, lay no claim either to antiquity, or to purity of linguistic form. Yet, as an authentic modern version, slightly colored by European teachings, of the ancient tribal traditions, it is well worth preservation. . . . The narrator was probably one of the native chiefs or priests, who had spent his life in the Ohio and Indiana towns of the Lenape, and who, though with some knowledge of Christian instruction, preferred the pagan rites, legends and myths of his ancestors. Probably certain lines and passages were repeated in the archaic form in which they had been handed down for generations. . . . Even to an ear not acquainted with the language, the chants of the 'Walam Olum' are obviously in metrical arrangement. The rhythm is syllabic and accentual, with frequent effort to select homophones (to which the correct form of the words is occasionally sacrificed), and sometimes alliteration. Iteration is also called in aid, and the metrical scheme is varied in the different chants." [27] Because of its great interest to the students of both Indian poetry and Indian history, the translation of the entire fragment is here given.

The "Walam Olum" provides many a point for discussion and debate, but most of these points have to do with questions of its authenticity or with matters of concern primarily to the student of folklore. The high-sounding roll of names of olden chiefs is dignified and impressive. The tone of the chronicle is gloomy and confused, and gives the impression of a serious and half-awakened people wandering in chaos. The effect is moving, in spite of the looseness and vagueness of many lines. The most poetic portion, without doubt, is the third section, which describes the wanderings of the tribe in search of a more temperate and comfortable climate, and is marked by the only noticeable poetic device in the entire fragment— the simple variation found in such lines as: "It freezes where they abode, it snows where they abode, it storms where they abode, it is cold where they abode."

THE WALAM OLUM OR RED SCORE [27]

At first, in that place, at all times, above the earth,
On the earth, was an extended fog, and there the great Manito was.
At first, forever, lost in space, everywhere, the great Manito was.

He made the extended land and the sky.
He made the sun, the moon, the stars.
He made them all to move evenly.
Then the wind blew violently, and it cleared, and the water flowed
    off far and strong.
And groups of islands grew newly, and there remained.
Anew spoke the great Manito, a manito to manitos,
To beings, mortals, souls and all,
And ever after he was a manito to men, and their grandfather.
He gave the first mother, the mother of beings.
He gave the fish, he gave the turtles, he gave the beasts, he gave the
    birds.
But an evil Manito made evil beings only, monsters;
He made the flies, he made the gnats.
All beings were then friendly.
Truly the manitos were active and kindly
To those very first men, and to those first mothers; fetched them
    wives,
And fetched them food, when first they desired it.
All had cheerful knowledge, all had leisure, all thought in gladness.
But very secretly an evil being, a mighty magician, came on earth,
And with him brought badness, quarreling, unhappiness,
Brought bad weather, brought sickness, brought death.
All this took place of old on the earth, beyond the great tide-water,
    at the first.

II

Long ago there was a mighty snake and beings evil to men.
This mighty snake hated those who were there and greatly disquieted
    those whom he hated.
They both did harm, they both injured each other, both were not
    in peace.
Driven from their homes they fought with this murderer.
The mighty snake firmly resolved to harm the men.
He brought three persons, he brought a monster, he brought a rush-
    ing water.
Between the hills the water rushed and rushed, dashing through and
    through, destroying much.

Nanabush [Manibozho], the Strong White One, grandfather of beings, grandfather of men, was on the Turtle Island.

There he was walking and creating, as he passed by and created the turtle.

Beings and men all go forth, they walk in the floods and shallow waters, downstream thither to the Turtle Island.

There were many monster fishes, which ate some of them.

The Manito daughter, coming, helped with her canoe, helped all, as they came and came.

And also Nanabush, Nanabush, the grandfather of all, the grandfather of beings, the grandfather of men, the grandfather of the turtle.

The men then were together on the turtle, like to turtles.

Frightened on the turtle, they prayed on the turtle that what was spoiled should be restored.

The water ran off, the earth dried, the lakes were at rest, all was silent, and the mighty snake departed.

III

After the rushing waters had subsided the Lenape of the turtle were close together, in hollow houses, living together there.

It freezes where they abode, it snows where they abode, it storms where they abode, it is cold where they abode.

At this northern place they speak favorably of mild, cool lands, with many deer and buffaloes.

As they journeyed, some being strong, some rich, they separated into house-builders and hunters;

The strongest, the most united, the purest, were the hunters.

The hunters showed themselves at the north, at the east, at the south, at the west.

In that ancient country, in that northern country, in that turtle country, the best of the Lenape were the Turtle men.

All the cabin fires of that land were disquieted, and all said to their priest, "Let us go."

To the Snake land to the east they went forth, going away, earnestly grieving.

Split asunder, weak, trembling, their land burned, they went, torn and broken, to the Snake Island.

Those from the north being free, without care, went forth from the
    land of snow, in different directions.
The fathers of the Bald Eagle and the White Wolf remain along the
    sea, rich in fish and mussels.
Floating up the streams in their canoes, our fathers were rich, they
    were in the light, when they were at those islands.
Head Beaver and Big Bird said, "Let us go to Snake Island," they said.
All say they will go along to destroy all the land.
Those of the north agreed,
Those of the east agreed,
Over the water, the frozen sea,
They went to enjoy it.
On the wonderful, slippery water,
On the stone-hard water all went,
On the great Tidal Sea, the mussel-bearing sea.
Ten thousand at night,
All in one night,
To the Snake Island, to the east, at night,
They walk and walk, all of them.
The men from the north, the east, the south,
The Eagle clan, the Beaver clan, the Wolf clan,
The best men, the rich men, the head men,
Those with wives, those with daughters, those with dogs,
They all come, they tarry at the land of the spruce pines;
Those from the west come with hesitation,
Esteeming highly their old home at the Turtle land.

IV

Long ago the fathers of the Lenape were at the land of spruce pines.
Hitherto the Bald Eagle band had been the pipe bearer,
While they were searching for the Snake Island, that great and fine
    land.
They having died, the hunters, about to depart, met together.
All say to Beautiful Head, "Be thou chief."
"Coming to the Snakes, slaughter at the Snake hill, that they leave it."
All of the Snake tribe were weak, and hid themselves in the Swampy
    Vales.
After Beautiful Head, White Owl was chief at Spruce Pine land.
After him, Keeping-Guard was chief of that people.

After him, Snow Bird was chief; he spoke of the south,
That our fathers should possess it by scattering abroad.
The Snake land was at the south, the great Spruce Pine land was
  toward the shore;
To the east was the Fish land, toward the lakes was the buffalo land.
After Snow Bird, the Seizer was chief, and all were killed,
The robbers, the snakes, the evil men, the stone men.

After the Seizer there were ten chiefs, and there was much warfare
  south and east.
After them, the Peaceable was chief at Snake land.
After him, Not-Black was chief, who was a straight man.
After him, Much-Loved was chief, a good man.
After him, No-Blood was chief, who walked in cleanliness.
After him, Snow-Father was chief, he of the big teeth.
After him, Tally-Maker was chief, who made records.
After him, Shiverer-with-Cold was chief, who went south to the corn
  land.
After him, Corn-Breaker was chief, who brought about the planting
  of corn.
After him, the Strong-Man was chief, who was useful to the chief-
  tains.
After him, the Salt-Man was chief; after him the Little-One was chief.
There was no rain, and no corn, so they moved further seaward.
At the place of caves, in the buffalo land, they at last had food, on a
  pleasant plain.
After the Little-One came the Fatigued; after him, the Stiff-One.
After him, the Reprover; disliking him, and unwilling to remain,
Being angry, some went off secretly, moving east.

The wise ones who remained made the Loving-One chief.
They settled again on the Yellow river, and had much corn on stone-
  less soil.
All being friendly, the Affable was chief, the first of that name.
He was very good, this Affable, and came as a friend to all the
  Lenape.

Again with the Tawa people, again with the Stone people, again with
    the northern people.
Grandfather-of-Boats was chief; he went to lands in boats.
Snow-Hunter was chief; he went to the north land.
Look-About was chief; he went to the Talega mountains.
East-Villager was chief; he was east of Talega.

A great land and a wide land was the east land,
A land without snakes, a rich land, a pleasant land.
Great Fighter was chief, toward the north.
At the Straight river, River-Loving was chief.
Becoming-Fat was chief at Sassafras land.
All the hunters made wampum again at the great sea.
Red-Arrow was chief at the stream again.
The Painted-Man was chief at the Mighty Water.
The Easterners and the Wolves go northeast.
Good-Fighter was chief, and went to the north.
The Mengwe, the Lynxes, all trembled.
Again an Affable was chief, and made peace with all.
All were friends, all were united, under this great chief.
Great-Beaver was chief, remaining in Sassafras land.
White-Body was chief on the sea shore.
Peace-Maker was chief, friendly to all.
He-Makes-Mistakes was chief, hurriedly coming.
At this time whites came on the Eastern sea.

Much-Honored was chief; he was prosperous.
Well-Praised was chief; he fought at the south.
He fought in the land of the Talega and Koweta.
White-Otter was chief; a friend of the Talamatans.
White-Horn was chief; he went to the Talega,
To the Hilini, to the Shawnees, to the Kanawhas.
Coming-as-a-Friend was chief; he went to the Great Lakes,
Visiting all his children, all his friends.
Cranberry-Eater was chief, friend of the Ottawas.
North-Walker was chief; he made festivals.
Slow-Gatherer was chief at the shore.

As three were desired, three those were who grew forth.
The Unami, the Minsi, the Chikini.
The Unami, the Minsi, the Chikini.
Man-Who-Fails was chief; he fought the Mengwe.
He-is-Friendly was chief; he scared the Mengwe.
Saluted was chief; thither,
Over there, on the Scioto, he had foes.
White-Crab was chief; a friend of the shore.
Watcher was chief; he looked toward the sea.
At this time, from north and south, the whites came.
They are peaceful; they have great things [ships]; who are they?

The Iroquois family has also produced a lengthy ritual that re-
cites its history. The tribes that settled in what is now New York
State formed a confederacy known as the "League of the Five
Nations," consisting of the Mohawks (Caniengas), Senecas, Oneidas,
Onondagas, and Cayugas; about 1715 their relatives the Tuscaroras
were admitted to limited membership, and thenceforward history
hears of the "Six Nations." The heart of this political organization
was a simplification of the old mourning ceremonies held at the death
of a chief. This "Rite of the Condoling Council" was a harmonizing
statement of the unity of the various tribes, an act of political as
well as religious faith, during which the roll of the chiefs was ut-
tered and the circumstances of the founding of the League recalled
in moving tones. Those circumstances centered around a name
familiar to us—the name of Hayenwatha or Hiawatha, the great re-
former and organizer of the League, who lived about the year 1500
A.D. and whose name Longfellow borrowed for his poem about an
entirely different tribe, the Chippewa.

Two Iroquois rituals have been translated by Horatio Hale from
written documents in the possession of the surviving chiefs charged
with carrying on these ancient ceremonies, which had been set down
in the Onondaga and Canienga dialects more than a century before
by white Protestant missionaries using a roman alphabet. The first
of these, the "Canienga Book," comprises the speeches addressed by
the representatives of the three "elder" nations of the confederacy
to the "younger" members whenever a chief of these younger tribes

is to be lamented. The "Onondaga Book," on the other hand, gives the ritual when a chief of the elder nations is mourned by the members of the younger nations. Both ceremonies consist of lengthy set speeches of considerable metaphorical content, in which are interspersed chants, prayers, and hymns; the verse is introduced in calling the roll of the villages belonging to the League and in listing the names of the chieftains who ruled in former days.

In the words of the translator: "This book, sometimes called the 'Book of the Condoling Council,' might properly enough be styled an Iroquois Veda. It comprises the speeches, songs, and other ceremonies which, from the earliest period of the confederacy, have composed the proceedings of their council when a deceased chief is lamented and his successor is installed in office. The fundamental laws of the league, a list of their ancient towns, and the names of the chiefs who constituted their first council, chanted in a kind of litany, are also comprised in the collection. . . . Instead of a race of rude and ferocious warriors, we find in this book a kindly and affectionate people, full of sympathy for their friends in distress, considerate to their women, tender to their children, anxious for peace, and imbued with a profound reverence for their constitution and its authors." [114]

The "Ancient Rites of the Condoling Council" began with a long prose address, which included the following hymn.

HYMN CALLED "HAIL" [114]

I come again to greet and thank the League;
I come again to greet and thank the kindred;
I come again to greet and thank the warriors;
I come again to greet and thank the women.
My forefathers,—what they established,—
My forefathers,—hearken to them!

During this rite, the speaker paid tribute to the chiefs who founded the Great League, and rolled out the tally of tribes and leaders. The first of the chiefs mentioned in the following famous chant from the "Canienga Book" is of course Shatekariwate or Hayenwatha (Hiawatha), "He-Who-Seeks-the-Wampum-Belt." In the version below have been substituted, for the jawbreaking literal transcriptions of native names in the original document, the translations found in Hale's notes.

RITES OF THE CONDOLING COUNCIL [114]

Woe! Woe!
Hearken ye!
We are diminished!
Woe! Woe!
The cleared land has become a thicket.
Woe! Woe!
The clear places are deserted.
Woe!
They are in their graves—
They who established it—
Woe!
The great League.
Yet they declared
It should endure—
The great League.
Woe!
Their work has grown old.
Woe!
Thus we are become miserable.

The Caniengas!
Continue to listen!
Thou who wert ruler,
He-Who-Seeks-the-Wampum-Belt!
That was the roll of you,
You who were joined in the work,
You who completed the work,
The Great League.

Continue to listen!
Thou who wert ruler,
He-Who-is-the-Loftiest-Tree!
Continue to listen!
Thou who wert ruler,
Double-Life!

Continue to listen!
Thou who wert ruler,
        Wide-Branches!
That was the roll of you,
You who were joined in the work,
You who completed the work,
The Great League.

Continue to listen!
Thou who wert ruler,
        Going-With-Two-Horns!
Continue to listen!
Thou who wert ruler,
        He-Puts-On-the-Rattles!
Continue to listen!
Thou who wert ruler,
        Great Wood-Drift!
That was the roll of you,
You who were joined in the work,
You who completed the work,
The Great League.

Ye two were principals,
Father and son,
Ye two completed the work,
The Great League.
Ye two aided each other,
Ye two founded the House.
Now, therefore, hearken!
Thou who wert ruler,
        Quiver-Bearer!
Continue to listen!
Thou who wert ruler,
        Rows-of-Ears-of-Corn!
Continue to listen!
Thou who wert ruler,
        Open-Voice!
That was the roll of you,
You who were joined in the work,

You who completed the work,
The Great League.

Continue to listen!
Thou who wert ruler,
    He-Has-a-Long-House!
Continue to listen!
Thou who wert ruler,
    Two-Branches!
Continue to listen!
Thou who wert ruler,
    He-Slides-Down!
That was the roll of you,
You who were joined in the work,
You who completed the work,
The Great League.

Continue to listen!
Thou who wert ruler,
    Two-Hanging-Ears!
Continue to listen!
Thou who wert ruler,
    Easy-Throat!
Continue to listen!
Thou who wert ruler,
    He-is-Buried!
That was the roll of you,
You who were joined in the work,
You who completed the work,
The Great League.

These were his uncles [the Onondagas]:
Now hearken!
Thou who wert ruler,
    Entangled One!
Continue to listen!
These were the cousins:
Thou who wert ruler,
    Best-Soil-Uppermost!
Continue to listen!

Thou who wert ruler,
    He-Looks-Both-Ways!
Continue to listen!
These were as brothers thenceforth:
Thou who wert ruler,
    Bitter Throat!
Continue to listen!
Thou who wert ruler,
    Journey's End!
Continue to listen!
Thou who wert ruler,
    Red Wings!
That was the roll of you.

These were his uncles,
Of the two clans:
    Voice Suspended!
    The Scattered One!
That was the roll of them!

These were as brothers thenceforth:
    [*name untranslated*]
    He-is-Bruised!
    He-Saw-Them!
This was the roll of you.

This befell
In ancient times,
They had their children,
Those the two clans.
He the high chief
    Hatchet-in-His-Belt!
This put away the clouds:
He was a war chief;
He was a high chief—
Acting in either office:
    [*name untranslated*]
This was the roll of you!

Then his son,
    He-Looks-Both-Ways!
With his brother,
    Coming-on-His-Knees!
This was the roll of you!

    Bruised One!
    Long Wampum-Belt!
    Puts-One-on-Another!
This was the roll of you.

Then they who are brothers:
    Touches-the-Sky!
    Doubly Cold!
    Mossy Place!
This was the roll of you!

    Crowding-Himself-In!
    Resting-On-It!
This was the roll of you!

Then his uncle,
    Beautiful Lake!
With his cousin,
    Skies-of-Equal-Length!
This was the roll of you!

    Withheld!
With his cousin,
    Large Forehead!
This was the roll of you!

    Threatened One!
With his cousin,—then
    The-Day-Fell-Down!
This was the roll of you!

Then, in later times,
They made additions
To the great mansion.
These were at the doorway,

They who were cousins,
These two guarded the doorway:
   Tangled Hair!
With his cousin,
   Open Door!
This was the roll of you!

Now we are dejected
In our minds.

Also from the Iroquois tribe came this ritual fragment from an initiation ceremony, translated by Harriet M. Converse:

DARKNESS SONG [37]
We wait in the darkness!
Come, all ye who listen,
Help in our night journey:
Now no sun is shining;
Now no star is glowing;
Come show us the pathway:
The night is not friendly;
She closes her eyelids;
The moon has forgot us,
We wait in the darkness!

The southern kindred of the Iroquois, the Cherokee tribe, who in their easily defended mountain fastnesses were able to practice the arts of peace long after the coming of the white man, developed a tribal civilization of a higher order. The rituals which have come down to us from among them are chiefly concerned with the use of charms for healing the sick and for working magic against enemies, witches, or unresponsive loved ones. These sacred chants have been closely studied by James Mooney, who collected a number of important manuscripts written in the Cherokee alphabet and translated them in two large monographs. This alphabet was invented by the celebrated Sequoya, whose father was a white man and whose name is immortalized in the giant trees of California.

"These formulas," says Mooney, "had been handed down orally from a remote antiquity until the early part of the present [nineteenth] century, when the invention of the Cherokee syllabary enabled the priests of the tribe to put them in writing. . . . The formulas here given, as well as those of the entire collection, were written out by the shamans themselves—men who adhere to the ancient religion and speak only their native language—in order that their sacred knowledge might be preserved in a systematic manner for their mutual benefit." [150] Not only are the formulas fascinating from a medical and anthropological viewpoint, but some of them show considerable poetic imagination. They may be closely compared to expressions of primitive medical theory in such English survivals as the Anglo-Saxon and medieval charms against toothache, against wens, and so on. Only a few of the large number of Mooney translations will here be given, to suggest the poetic thought devoted by the Cherokee to healing acts and to obtaining success in various other ventures.

The following formula for obtaining long life could be recited either by the medicine man or the client himself.

FORMULA FOR OBTAINING LONG LIFE [151]

Now, then!
Ha, now thou hast come to listen, thou Long Human Being, thou art
    staying, thou Helper of human beings.
Thou never lettest go thy grasp from the soul.
Thou hast, as if it were, taken a firmer grasp upon the soul.
I originated at the cataract, not so far away.
I will stretch out my hand to where thou art.
My soul has come to bathe itself in thy body.
The white foam will cling to my head as I walk along the path of
    life, the white staff will come into my extended hand.
The fire of the hearth will be left burning for me incessantly.
The soul has been lifted up successively to the seventh upper world.

The following charm was used to accompany treatment for a disease of young children. "The disease is declared to have been caused by birds, it being asserted in the first paragraph that a bird has cast its shadow upon the sufferer, while in the second it is declared that they have gathered in council (in his body)."

FORMULA FOR YOUNG CHILDREN [150]

Yu! Listen!

Quickly you have drawn near to hearken, O Blue Sparrow-Hawk; in
    the spreading treetops you are at rest.

Quickly you have come down.

The intruder is only a bird which has overshadowed him.

Swiftly you have swooped down upon it.

Relief is accomplished.

Yu!

Yu! Listen!

Quickly you have drawn near to hearken, O Brown Rabbit-Hawk;
    you are at rest there above.

Ha! Swiftly now you have come down.

It is only the birds which have come together for a council.

Quickly you have come and scattered them.

Relief is accomplished.

Yu!

Another charm, for advancing parturition, gives an idea of the
curious family relationships of the tribe. "In this formula for child-
birth, the idea is to frighten the child and coax it to come, by telling
it, if a boy, that an ugly old woman is coming, or if a girl, that her
grandfather is coming only a short distance away. The reason of this
lies in the fact that an old woman is the terror of all the little boys of
the neighborhood, constantly teasing and frightening them by de-
claring that she means to live until they grow up and then compel
one of them to marry her. For the same reason the maternal grand-
father, who is always a privileged character in the family, is especially
dreaded by the little girls. As the sex is an uncertain quantity, the
possible boy is always first addressed in the formulas, and if no re-
sult seems to follow, the doctor then concludes that the child is a
girl and addresses her in similar tones." [150] Another childbirth charm
in the same volume carries the idea that the child, if a boy, can be
enticed by the promise of the gift of a bow; if a girl, a meal-sifter is
offered to the one who can get it first.

THIS IS TO MAKE CHILDREN JUMP DOWN [150]

Listen!
You little man, get up now at once.
There comes an old woman.
The horrible old thing is coming, only a little way off.
Listen! Quick!
Get your bed and let us run away.
Yu!

Listen!
You little woman, get up now at once.
There comes your grandfather.
The horrible old fellow is coming only a little way off.
Listen! Quick!
Get your bed and let us run away.
Yu!

Here is a formula by which the shaman seeks to drive away a storm which threatens to injure the young corn. The storm—which is not directly named—is addressed and declared to be coming on like a raging animal in the rutting season. The shaman then seeks to misdirect the storm by pointing out that the storm's wife has taken a path leading to the upper regions, and begs the storm-spirit to follow her to the treetops of the lofty mountains and away from the cultivated fields.

TO FRIGHTEN A STORM [151]

Listen!
O now you are coming in rut. Ha!
I am exceedingly afraid of you.
But yet you are only tracking your wife.
Her footprints can be seen there directed upward toward the heavens.
I have pointed them out for you.
Let your paths stretch out along the treetops on the lofty mountains
    and you shall have them [the paths] lying down without being
    disturbed.
Let your path as you go along be where the waving branches meet.
Listen!

The Cherokees, like many another social group in history, believed that disease was frequently caused by spells put upon the patient by a witch. The witch was commonly supposed to go about under cover of darkness, and hence was called "the night-goer." "As the counteracting of a deadly spell," remarks Mooney, "always results in the death of its author, the formula is stated to be not merely to drive away the wizard, but to kill him, or, according to the formulistic expression, 'to shorten him (his life) on this side.' " [150]

TO SHORTEN A NIGHT-GOER ON THIS SIDE [150]

Listen!
In the Frigid Land above, you repose, O Red Man.
Quickly we two have prepared your arrows for the soul of the
    Imprecator.
He has them lying along the path.
Quickly we two will take his soul as we go along.

Listen!
In the Frigid Land above, you repose, O Purple Man.
Ha! Quickly now we two have prepared your arrows for the soul
    of the Imprecator.
He has them lying along the path.
Quickly we two will cut his soul in two.

The incantations of the members of the southern Muskhogean family, through whose country Hernando De Soto's expedition passed in 1540, are not widely different from those of the Cherokees. Both the Choctaws of Mississippi and the Creeks of Alabama were great singers in the old days, but most of their songs are now gone.

Two curing songs from the Creek tribe will be given. The following, translated by Speck, was supposed to be a cure for aching teeth and gums and swollen cheeks, ailments which were attributed to the baneful influence of the water moccasin.

SNAKE MEDICINE SONG [183]

In the path he was coiled up.
On a long stick he was coiled up.
On the edge of the water he was coiled up.

Around a tree branch he was coiled, it is said.
On a hollow tree he was coiled up.
He hisses continuously.
Lying, he made a noise.
Stone is in the grass
Here coiled up.
Lying, he made a noise.
On a long stick
Here coiled up.
Lying, he made a noise.
In the sunny path
Here coiled up.
          Hiss!

Another, translated by Swanton, was also a cure for a disease presumed to have been caused by a snake.

MEDICINE SONG FOR SNAKE SICKNESS [192]

O, spirit of the white fox, come.
O, spirit of the white fox, come.
O, spirit of the white fox, come.
O, hater of snakes, come.
Snakes who have hurt this man, come.
Come, O white fox, and kill this snake.

O, spirit of the red fox, come, etc.
O, spirit of the black fox, come, etc.

The Creeks were supposed to have learned many songs from the neighboring Choctaws. In William Bartram's celebrated *Travels* (1792), when speaking of the Creeks, we find: "Some of their most favorite songs and dances, they have from their enemies, the Choctaws; for it seems these people are very eminent for poetry and music; every town amongst them strives to excel each other in composing new songs for dances; and by a custom amongst them, they must give at least one new song, for exhibition, at every annual busk." Among the Choctaws of today, however, Miss Densmore has found comparatively few songs, and the words of most are few and simple. The following is a sample of a Choctaw hunting song:

GO AND GRIND SOME CORN [58]

Go and grind some corn, we will go camping.
Go and sew, we will go camping.
I passed on and you were sitting there crying.
You were lazy and your hoe is rusty.

The medicine songs of the Chippewa tribe around the Great
Lakes, although their magical ideas are similar to those in other
Indian groups, are rather different in form. Among them has
existed for a long time a grand medicine society called the Midé-
wiwin, to which both men and women belonged, and part of whose
ceremonies were concerned with healing. These Midé songs, which
were recalled to the singer's memory by sketches on birch bark, are
usually brief. A number of them refer to the sacred symbols of the
society, such as the shell or the totemic animals, and the translations
are likely to be cryptic or else to sound commonplace. Many of
them have been translated by H. R. Schoolcraft, Frances Densmore,
and W. J. Hoffman. Here are a few of these symbolic songs from
Schoolcraft's volume of 1851:

MIDÉ SONGS: SCHOOLCRAFT [175]

What! my life, my single tree!—we dance around you.

All around the circle of the sky I hear the Spirit's voice.

I walk upon half of the sky.

I am the crow—I am the crow—his skin is my body.

A few collected by Hoffman may also be cited:

MIDÉ SONGS: HOFFMAN [122]

The Spirit placed medicine in the ground; let us take it.

I have the medicine in my heart.

Yes, there is much medicine you may cry for.

I am as strong as the bear.

A number of excellent Midé songs are found in Miss Densmore's
studies of Chippewa music. The first one is of structural as well as
symbolic interest.

THE SKY CLEARS [56]

Verily
The sky clears
When my Midé drum
Sounds
For me.
Verily
The waters are smooth
When my Midé drum
Sounds
For me.

THIRD INITIATION SONG [56]

There comes a sound
From my medicine bag.

THE SOUND IS FADING AWAY [56]

The sound is fading away.
It is of five sounds.
Freedom.
The sound is fading away.
It is of five sounds.

Many of the Chippewa songs reveal a knowledge of nature in many of its aspects, a knowledge which derived from the Indian habit, born of necessity, of scanning his environment with eyes that missed nothing. It should be said, however, that there are almost no poems to be found in the translations from many tribes which reflect in a lyrical manner the delight in nature for its own sake. The sort of white-man poetry exemplified by Wordsworthian passages which merely describe "scenery" in picturesque phrases cannot be found among the North American Indians. In the slightest natural oddity the Indian might find a means of winning power over unseen forces, or a practical life lesson, or the stuff of myth; but it was foreign to him to scan a landscape seeking literary raw material. Purely descriptive verse would have seemed to him to serve no useful function. It was important to know one's surroundings and to remark all the details of the lives of the creatures who shared the earth with one; but poetry was for a very definite purpose, and comment without

a motive—no matter how clever the word-spinning might be—
would be idle. Hence we find that some of the best Indian observa-
tions on nature are in prayers, ceremonials, and medicine songs, and
are designed to influence nature rather than to describe it. Although
a number of the Chippewa verses here given portray natural scenes,
they are songs which have the chief purpose of "making medicine."

This Chippewa song gives a fresh impression of the coming of
June days:

SPRING SONG [57]
As my eyes search the prairie
I feel the summer in the spring.

This Midé song describes the distant sounds of the village during
pauses in the initiation ceremony of this society:

THE NOISE OF THE VILLAGE [57]
Whenever I pause—
The noise
Of the village.

A number of other Chippewa songs might seem to the casual reader
to be lyrical in spirit.

THE SKY WILL RESOUND [57]
It will resound finely,
The sky,
When I come making a noise.

MAPLE SUGAR [57]
Maple sugar
Is the only thing
That satisfies me.

SONG OF THE THUNDERS [56]
Sometimes I,
I go about pitying
Myself
While I am carried by the wind
Across the sky.

SONG OF THE TREES [56]
The wind
Only
I am afraid of.

MY MUSIC REACHES TO THE SKY [56]
My music
Reaches
To the sky.

Comprehension of such songs is often greatly aided by an understanding of Indian customs and beliefs. The following sketch of the approach of a thunderstorm is explained by the translator thus: "The Thunder *manido* represents to the Indian the mysterious spirit of the storm, and he imagines that this *manido* sometimes makes a noise to warn him of its approach. This is his interpretation of the distant thunder which precedes a storm. Hearing this, the Indian hastens to put tobacco on the fire in order that the smoke may ascend as an offering or signal of peace to the *manido*. The idea which underlies the song is, 'That which lives in the sky is coming and, being friendly, it makes a noise to let me know of its approach.' This means much less to the white race than to the Indian. We are accustomed to noise; the Indian habitually approaches in silence, unless he wishes to announce his presence." [56]

THE APPROACH OF THE STORM [56]
From the half
Of the sky
That which lives there
Is coming, and makes a noise.

Among the Indians of earlier days there were few love songs expressing a sentimental attachment between the sexes. This subordination of a poetic theme which has been common in European and Oriental poetry is one of the chief characteristics of American Indian verse. Except for the "love-charm," which was always allied with an evil intention in the mind of the Indian, there is very little to show that he frequently sang about romantic love. There are a few songs in which the women promise to be true while the loved one is on the warpath, and among certain tribes, such as the Eskimos or the more promiscuous groups of the Northwest Coast, there are references to personal affection or longing; but even among the effete Aztecs and Mayas of Mexico there was little glorification of domestic or romantic love.

The best commentator upon Indian love songs is Miss Densmore, who has studied the music of many widely scattered tribal groups. Her observations are worth quoting rather fully:

"It is probable that the world would not have reached its present interest in Indian music if our artists had not sung Indian love songs, and yet the writer has been repeatedly informed that songs concerning the passion of love were not sung by the old-time Indians except in the working of 'love charms.' . . . Mention has been made of the use of songs in working magic and attracting a person of the opposite sex. This custom does not seem to have prevailed in all tribes and was not favorably regarded. Such a song, accompanied by the use of some 'charm,' was generally used for an evil purpose and has nothing to do with the love song of the present time. My Papago interpreter said: 'Love songs are dangerous. If a man gets to singing them we send for a medicine man to treat him and make him stop.' . . . Among the Chippewa and Menominee it is said that love songs are modern and are usually associated with disappointment or intoxication. The development of the modern love song appears to have been greatest in tribes living in close contact with the fringes of civilization. It is admitted that there are many love songs on Indian reservations at the present time. They are plaintive melodies and some of them approach more nearly to our idea of Indian music than the genuine old melodies of the race. . . . The writer has studied this phase of Indian music chiefly among the Chippewa and Menominee and the words of their love songs are forlorn, expressing disappointment rather than affection. There are also taunting songs and others concerning harsh words and quarrels. All this is in strong contrast to the quiet dignity and poetry of the old songs." [54]

The following are given by Miss Densmore as typical words of modern love songs from the two tribes mentioned:

CHIPPEWA LOVE SONGS [54]

I sit here thinking of her;
I am sad as I think of her.

Come, I beseech you, let us sing;
Why are you offended?

I do not care for you any more;
Someone else is in my thoughts.

You desire vainly that I seek you;
The reason is, I come to see your younger sister.

Come, let us drink.

Three more are from the Menominee tribe:

MENOMINEE LOVE SONGS [54]

At some future time you will think of me and cry,
My sweetheart.

You had better go home,
Your mother loves you so much.

O my! How that girl loves me—
The one I am secretly courting.

The most interesting love song in Miss Densmore's collection, according to her judgment, was given her by a Chippewa woman who died in 1926 at about the age of ninety-one.

A LOON I THOUGHT IT WAS [54]

A loon I thought it was,
But it was my love's splashing oar.
To Sault Ste. Marie he has departed,
My love has gone on before me,
Never again can I see him.
A loon I thought it was,
But it was my love's splashing oar.

Another song of longing also comes from the Chippewas:

WHEN I THINK OF HIM [56]
Although he said it
Still
I am filled with longing
When I think of him.

Here are three samples of magical love-charms from the Chippewas:

LOVE-CHARMS [56]
What are you saying to me?
I am arrayed like the roses
And beautiful as they.

I can charm the man.
He is completely fascinated by me.

In the center of the earth
Wherever he may be
Or under the earth.

One of the earliest love songs to be translated was given by Schoolcraft. It was sung at night by the lover of a Chippewa girl as he approached her dwelling. Each verse was repeated several times, in the hope that the girl would agree to the sentiments of the serenade and welcome the singer to her lodge.

I WILL WALK [175]
I will walk into somebody's dwelling,
Into somebody's dwelling will I walk.

To thy dwelling, my dearly beloved,
Some night will I walk, will I walk.

Some night in the winter, my beloved,
To thy dwelling will I walk, will I walk.

This very night, my beloved,
To thy dwelling will I walk, will I walk.

Another Chippewa love song is given by Schoolcraft in his historical volume:

IT IS MY FORM AND PERSON [175]

It is my form and person that makes me great.
Hear the voice of my song—it is my voice.
I shield myself with secret coverings.
All your thoughts are known to me—blush!
I could draw you hence, were you on a distant island;
Though you were on the other hemisphere.
I speak to your naked heart.

A plaintive song, taken from the legend of an Algonkin girl
marooned by jealous rivals on an island, was translated by John
Reade from the Wabanaki dialect of eastern Canada.

NOW I AM LEFT [163]

Now I am left on this lonely island to die—
No one to hear the sound of my voice.
Who will bury me when I die?
Who will sing my death-song for me?
My false friends leave me here to die alone;
Like a wild beast, I am left on this island to die.
I wish the wind spirit would carry my cry to my love!
My love is as swift as the deer; he would speed through the forest
    to find me;
Now I am left on this lonely island to die.
I wish the spirit of air would carry my breath to my love.
My love's canoe, like the sunlight, would shoot through the water to
    my side;
But I am left on this lonely island to die, with no one to pity me but
    the little birds.
My love is brave and strong; but, when he hears my fate, his stout
    heart will break;
And I am on this lonely island to die.
Now the night comes on, and all is silent but the owl.
He sings a mournful song to his mate, in pity for me.
I will try to sleep.
I wish the night spirit to hear my song; he will tell my love of my
    fate; and when I awake, I shall see the one I love.
I am on this lonely island to die.

War songs as well as love songs survive in the eastern areas. A war song of the Passamaquoddy tribe of Maine is given by J. Walter Fewkes, who states that the words of many of these songs are improvised, but that the tunes are ancient.

PASSAMAQUODDY WAR SONG [89]

I will arise with my tomahawk in my hand, and I must have revenge on that nation which has slain my poor people.
I arise with war club in my hand, and follow the bloody track of that nation which killed my people.
I will sacrifice my own life and the lives of my warriors.
I arise with war club in my hand, and follow the track of my enemy.
When I overtake him I will take his scalp and string it on a long pole, and I will stick it in the ground, and my warriors will dance around it for many days; then I will sing my song for the victory over my enemy.

Understanding of the following Cherokee ritual war song, recorded by Mooney, depends upon knowing the color symbolism of that tribe—a system which is not far off from our own. Red, the color of the war club, is symbolic of success and has no reference to blood. Black, of course, is a sign of evil, death, and mourning. White, as a symbol of peace, is here noted as incongruous, and the translator believes the war-whoop should be red. Blue, as in our slang term, is emblematic of failure, disappointment, dejection, or unsatisfied desire.

CHEROKEE WAR SONG [150]

Hayi! Yu! Listen!
Now instantly we have lifted up the red war club.
Quickly his soul shall be without motion.
There under the earth, where the black war clubs shall be moving about like ball sticks in the game, there his soul shall be, never to reappear.
We cause it to be so.
He shall never go and lift up the war club.
We cause it to be so.
There under the earth the black war club and the black fog have come together as one for their covering.

It shall never move about [i.e., the black fog shall never be lifted
    from them].
We cause it to be so.

Instantly shall their souls be moving about there in the seventh
    heaven.
Their souls shall never break in two.
So shall it be.

Quickly we have moved them [their souls] on high for them, where
    they shall be going about in peace.
You have shielded yourselves with the red war clubs.
Their souls shall never be knocked about.
Cause it to be so.
There on high their souls shall be going about.
Let them shield themselves with the white war-whoop.
Instantly grant that they shall never become blue.
Yu!

A number of war songs translated by Schoolcraft have historical
interest, since they were among the first to be put into English.

HEAR MY VOICE [175]

Hear my voice, Birds of War!
I prepare a feast for you to feed on;
I see you cross the enemy's lines;
Like you I shall go.
I wish the swiftness of your wings;
I wish the vengeance of your claws;
I muster my friends;
I follow your flight.
Ho, you young men warriors,
Bear your angers to the place of fighting!

HERE ON MY BREAST [175]

Here on my breast have I bled!
See—see! My battle scars!
Ye mountains, tremble at my yell!

I strike for life.

I AM RISING [175]

I am rising to seek the warpath.
The earth and the sky are before me.
I walk by day and by night,
And the evening star is my guide.

The following song is found in two different versions:

FROM THE SOUTH: I [175]

From the south they come,
The birds, the warlike birds,
    With sounding wings.

I wish to change myself
To the body of that swift bird.

I throw away my body in the strife.

FROM THE SOUTH: II [175]

From the south they came, Birds of War—
Hark! to their passing scream.
I wish the body of the fiercest,
As swift, as cruel, as strong.
I cast my body to the chance of fighting.
Happy shall I be to lie in that place,
In that place where the fight was,
Beyond the enemy's line.

Another was given by Schoolcraft in both a free and a metrical
version:

THE BATTLE-BIRDS [175]

The battle-birds swoop from the sky,
They thirst for the warrior's heart;
They look from their circles on high,
And scorn every flesh but the brave.

(Metrical version)

The eagles scream on high,
They whet their forked beaks;
Raise—raise the battle cry,
'Tis fame our leader seeks.

Songs of war from the same tribe were collected by Miss Densmore more than half a century later. One of these commemorates the deeds of the warriors in a battlefield beside a river, and is said to have been composed during the fight.

ON THE BANK OF A STREAM [57]
Across the river
They speak of me as being.

The composer of this war song was a warrior named Butterfly:

THE SONG OF BUTTERFLY [57]
In the coming heat
Of the day
I stood there.

This is the death-song of a warrior following a victory over the Sioux:

DEATH-SONG OF NAMEBINES [57]
The odor of death,
I discern the odor of death
In the front of my body.

This song accompanied a war-dance in which the actions of animals were imitated.

SONG OF THE BUFFALO [57]
Strike ye
Our land
With curved horns.

Finally, a striking but simple bit of imagery is found in the glorification of the war-arrow:

ARROW SONG [57]
Scarlet
Is its head.

A few songs for children have been discovered in the eastern areas. This song from Schoolcraft might well have been reflected in Longfellow's *Hiawatha*:

CHIPPEWA CRADLE SONG [176]

Who is this?
Who is this?
Giving light [the light of the eye]
On the top of my lodge.

It is I—the little owl,
    Coming,
It is I—the little owl,
    Coming,
Down! Down!

The following cradle song from the Creek tribe is given in both a free and a literal translation. It was supposed to have been heard by a hunter who, while passing a bear's den, listened to the advice the old she-bear gave to her cubs.

CREEK CRADLE SONG [193]
(Literal translation)

Down the stream
You hear the noise of her going
That is what they say
Up the stream
Running unseen
Running unseen
Up the stream
You hear the noise of her going
That is what they say
To the top of the bald peak
Running unseen
Running unseen

(Free translation)

If you hear the noise of the chase
Going down the stream
Then run up the stream.
If you hear the noise of the chase
Going up the stream
Then run to the top of the bald peak,
Then run to the top of the bald peak.

A curious orgiastic form of social dancing and singing took place among the Creek tribe. "One of the favorite Creek dances is the Crazy Dance," writes the translator, Dr. Speck, "so named because the participants behave like wild people, men and women taking freedom with each other's persons and acting in general in such a way as to provoke mirth." [183] These licentious songs were purely secular, and although originally each was the work of one or at least a few composers, the verses were not spontaneous, for they were sung by a leader with chorus responses from the dancers. The boasting tone reminds us of some of the vainglorious chants from the Eskimos or the Pacific Northwest tribes.

CRAZY DANCE [183]

My mule, saddle him for me,
On the prairie big, when we get there,
Buffalo young bull, when I kill him,
My wife's mother, when we eat together,
When she scolds me. Osage chief,
When I become his son-in-law, many little Osages,
When I made them.
Morning star big, when it is rising,
Old turkey gobbler. When I hear him gobbling
My old gun, I start with it on my shoulder.
I'll go along, when I get there,
On tree limb big, I'll see him.
On a tree standing, I'll see him.
I'll aim at him; I'll shoot him.
When I shoot him, I'll kill him, turning. My wife's mother,
I'll take it on my back. When I get there
My sisters-in-law, turkey breast meat,
When we eat it together, when they begin quarreling,
Fighting with each other, I'll knock them about.
I'll eat it all up myself. *Whoop!*

≋ 7 ≋

MAYAS AND AZTECS OF ANCIENT MEXICO

THE HIGHEST pre-Columbian civilizations in North America
were those of the Mayas, of southern Mexico and northern Central
America, and the Nahua tribes of the Aztec "empire," made familiar
to us through the pages of Prescott. At the time of the conquest of
Mexico in 1521 by Hernando Cortés, the Mayas were in the last
stages of decline after two thousand years of a great artistic culture,
and the conqueror accomplished the downfall of the military state
set up by the Aztecs, who had centered their political and military
conquests at the island-city of Tenochtitlán in the Valley of Mexico
two hundred years earlier and had taken over many of the culture
traits of the Mayas and the earlier invading Nahua tribes of the
region. Both the Mayas and Aztecs had written literatures which
were part of a nobleman's education, paid honor to poets who com-
posed songs for many occasions, and gave public performances at
which the recitation of verses was featured.

The most imposing ruins in the New World bear testimony to the
greatness of the Mayan race, whose history, according to computa-
tions based on their excellent reckonings of time, goes back to about
200 B.C. Their jungle cities of worked stone, carved in relief with
intricate sculptures, represent a civilization that reached its height

in the sixth century. They practiced intensive agriculture, raising corn, beans, peppers, and cacao; wove fine cotton cloth; used large canoes; and were pre-eminent in architecture, art, astronomical knowledge, and the use of a precise calendar.

The Aztecs, like other tribes of central Mexico, were inheritors of the Mayan culture, and surpassed the Mayas only in the use of copper tools and in the devastating art of organized warfare. From their legendary place of origin, the "Seven Caves," which was probably in the deserts of our west, the Aztecs descended southward as the seventh of the waves of invading Nahua barbarians to sweep into the central valley of Mexico. The Aztecs or Mexicans, the Romans of the New World, set up their capital in 1325 at Tenochtitlán, on the ruins of which Mexico City now stands. From this citadel they conquered first one and then another surrounding tribe and united them all into a strong confederacy. Gradually these warriors absorbed the culture previously developed by the Mayas, the Toltecs, and other earlier inhabitants of the area, and in two hundred years rose to the domination that collapsed only when Cortés leveled Montezuma's city brick by brick. Aztec culture traits, similar to those of the Mayas, reveal a high appreciation of the arts and of social organization. They were skillful builders of palaces and pyramids, and their capital city had canals, aqueducts, markets, aviaries, and a zoological garden. They made gold filigree and ornaments of gold, silver, and copper cast in molds of wax, charcoal, and clay; tools of copper and tin; fine feather and stone mosaics; carvings of obsidian and jadeite; good pottery; finely woven cloth of cotton and agave cactus fibers, excellently dyed; and books on parchment and agave paper. They cultivated corn, beans, peppers, gourds, cotton, fruits, and the cactus plant, which supplied them with many products, including pulque or cactus beer. Their highly organized government maintained armies of skilled soldiers, who went forth in magnificent costumes and plumed helmets, bearing decorated shields and flint-toothed clubs. The social order bestowed definite property rights; their society consisted of nobles, common people trained for many trades, and slaves. The powerful priesthood directed education and ran the elaborate religious system, which consisted of regular rituals and ceremonial sacrifices; the children of common people as well as nobles were educated in schools for both boys and girls. The Nahuas were almost the only North American tribe to cultivate poetry as an art of pure entertainment. The profession of poet stood in high honor; many companies of singers and dancers were maintained; schools were carried on to teach the art of singing; and large public performances were an important part of their lives. The distinction between composers of songs and those who sang them was clearly kept.

Few Indian poems from Mexico, aside from those of the Mayas and Aztecs, have been translated into English. The main translators in this area are Daniel G. Brinton, Herbert J. Spinden, H. B. Alexander, G. T. Smisor, and Ralph L. Roys.

The Mayas, according to Diego de Landa, a Spanish writer of 1565, practised the art of "reading and writing their books with characters which were written, and pictures which represented the things written. They wrote their books on a large sheet doubled into folds, which was afterwards inclosed between two boards, which they decorated handsomely. They were written from side to side. in columns, as they were folded. They manufactured this paper from the root of a tree and gave it a white surface on which one could write." [26] Most of the treasures of Mayan literature have been lost, because of the wide destruction of the ancient codices and because the key to interpretation of most of their written characters has not been worked out. The main source of Mayan poetry that survives is the "Books of Chilan Balan," native chronicles of the Yucatan villages which were supposed to have been the prophecies of a native soothsayer and which were written in roman script shortly after the Conquest and secretly preserved.

The following prophecy of Chilan, according to Brinton, the translator, dates from the fifteenth century.

RECITAL OF THE PRIEST CHILAN [23]

Eat, eat, while there is bread,
Drink, drink, while there is water;
A day comes when dust shall darken the air,
When a blight shall wither the land,

When a cloud shall arise,
When a mountain shall be lifted up,
When a strong man shall seize the city,
When ruin shall fall upon all things,
When the tender leaf shall be destroyed,
When eyes shall be closed in death;
When there shall be three signs on a tree,
Father, son and grandson hanging dead on the same tree;
When the battle flag shall be raised,
And the people scattered abroad in the forests.

Brinton gives elsewhere another Mayan premonitory chant by a priest who foresaw evil to his nation; it is dated about the year 1469.

PROPHECY OF PECH, PRIEST OF CHICHEN-ITZÁ [26]

Ye men of Itzá, hearken to the tidings,
Listen to the forecast of this cycle's end;
Four have been the ages of the world's progressing,
Now the fourth is ending, and its end is near.
A mighty lord is coming, see you give him honor;
A potent lord approaches, to whom all must bow;
I, the prophet, warn you, keep in mind my boding,
Men of Itzá, mark it, and await your lord.

A fragment of verse from the Maya "Prophecies of the Katuns" is given by Spinden, with a few modifications of the original translation by Roys. This poem of the post-Cortés period keenly indicts the militant Christianity of the conquest by an excursion into irony: "Tribute was introduced on a large scale, and Christianity was introduced on a large scale."

FROM THE PROPHECY OF KATUN 9 AHAU (1556–1575) [186]

Then began the building of the church
Here in the center of Tihoo;
Great labor is the destiny of the katun.
Then began execution by hanging,
And the fire at the ends of their hands.
Then also came ropes and cords into the world.
Then came the children of the younger brothers

Under the hardship of legal summons and tribute.
Tribute was introduced on a large scale,
And Christianity was introduced on a large scale.
Then the seven sacraments of God's word were established.
Receive your guests heartily; our elder brothers come!

A few chronicles from Central America exist which reveal poetic imagination and occasionally a semblance of poetic form. Poetic elements may be found even in a document as prosaic as a legal brief. In the "Annals of the Cakchiquels," the purpose of which was to establish the land rights of a family of Guatemala, the Spanish grant, as translated by Brinton, begins with a lengthy recital of the tribal creation myth, of which this quotation is a sample: "And the Obsidian Stone is brought forth by the precious Xibalbay, the glorious Xibalbay; and man is made by the Maker, the Creator. The Obsidian Stone was his sustainer when man was made in misery and when man was formed; he was fed with wood, he was fed with leaves; he wished only the earth, he could not speak, he could not walk; he had no blood, he had no flesh; so say our fathers, our ancestors, O ye my sons." [24]

The "Popul Vuh," the sacred book of the Quiché tribe of Guatemala, is a consciously literary document which was probably composed originally in verse. It was put into writing in the seventeenth century and translated into Spanish by Francisco Ximenes. One example of its many passages of highly imaginative diction is found in H. B. Alexander's English rendering of the first part of the Quiché Genesis:

FROM THE POPUL VUH [2]

Admirable is the account of the time in which it came to pass that all was formed in heaven and upon earth, the quartering of their signs, their measure and alignment, and the establishment of parallels to the skies and upon the earth to the four quarters thereof, as was spoken by the Creator and Maker, the Mother, the Father of life and of all existence, that one by whom all move and breathe, father and sustainer of the peace of peoples, by whose wisdom was premeditated the excellence of all that doth exist in the heavens, upon the earth, in lake and sea.

Lo, all was suspense, all was calm and silent; all was motionless, all was quiet, and wide was the immensity of the skies.

Lo, the first word and the first discourse.

There was not yet a man; not an animal; there were no birds nor fish; there was no wood, no stone, no bog, no ravine, neither vegetation nor marsh; only the sky existed.

The face of the earth was not yet to be seen; only the peaceful sea and the expanse of the heavens.

Nothing was yet formed into a body; nothing was joined to another thing; naught held itself poised; there was not a rustle, not a sound beneath the sky.

There was naught that stood upright; there were only the quiet waters of the sea, solitary within its bounds; for as yet naught existed.

There were only immobility and silence in the darkness and in the night.

Alone was the Creator, the Maker, Tepeu, the Lord, and Gucumatz, the Plumed Serpent, those who engender, those who give being, alone upon the waters like a growing light.

They are enveloped in green and azure, whence is the name Gucumatz, and their being is great wisdom.

Lo, how the sky existeth, how the Heart of the Sky existeth—for such is the name of God, as He doth name Himself!

It is then that the word came to Tepeu and to Gucumatz, in the shadows and in the night, and spake with Tepeu and with Gucumatz. And they spake and consulted and meditated, and they joined their words and their counsels.

Then light came while they consulted together; and at the moment of dawn man appeared while they planned concerning the production and increase of the groves and of the climbing vines, there in the shade and in the night, through that one who is the Heart of the Sky, whose name is Hurakan.

The Lightning is the first sign of Hurakan; the second is the Streak of Lightning; the third is the Thunderbolt which striketh; and these three are the Heart of the Sky.

Then they came to Tepeu, to Gucumatz, and held counsel touching civilized life; how seed should be formed, how light should be produced, how the sustainer and nourisher of all.

"Let it be thus done.

"Let the waters retire and cease to obstruct, to the end that earth exist here, that it harden itself and show its surface, to the end that it be sown, and that the light of day shine in the heavens and upon the earth; for we shall receive neither glory nor honor from all that we have created and formed until human beings exist, endowed with sentience."

Thus they spake while the earth was formed by them.

It is thus, veritably, that creation took place, and the earth existed.

"Earth," they said, and immediately it was formed.

Like a fog or a cloud was its formation into the material state, when, like great lobsters, the mountains appeared upon the waters, and in an instant there were great mountains.

Only by marvelous power could have been achieved this their resolution when the mountains and the valleys instantly appeared with groves of cypress and pine upon them.

Then was Gucumatz filled with joy.

"Thou art welcome, O Heart of the Sky, O Hurakan, O Streak of Lightning, O Thunderbolt!"

"This that we have created and shaped will have its end," they replied.

And thus first were formed the earth, the mountains, and the plains; and the course of the waters was divided, the rivulets running serpentine among the mountains; it is thus that the waters existed when the great mountains were unveiled.

Thus was accomplished the creation of the earth when it was formed by those who are the Heart of the Sky and the Heart of the Earth; for so those are called who first made fruitful the heaven and the earth while yet they were suspended in the midst of the waters.

Such was its fecundation when they fecundated it while its fulfillment and its composition were meditated by them.

Probably the oldest fragments of New World literature, according to the translator Spinden, are the Nahua laments for the great Toltec captains that flourished in the twelfth and thirteenth centuries, who drove the Mayas from Chichen-Itzá and were in turn forced by the Aztecs to abandon their home at Teotihuacan. "Tollan" was the Golden Age homeplace of the Toltec tribe.

TOLTEC LAMENT [186]

In Tollan, alas! stood the House of Beams,
Where still the serpent columns stand.
But Nacxitl, our noble lord, has departed,
He has gone into the far country
(Already our lamented princes have departed!)
And there in the Red Land he is undone.
In Cholula we were when we set forth
For Poyautecatitlan to cross the water in boats:
The wept-for ones have departed!
I have come to the foreign boundaries,
I, Ihuiquecholli, I, Mamaliteuchtli:
I am sad, for my lord Ihuitimalli is gone.
He deserts me, I who am Matlacxochitl.
Weep, weep! O, weep, weep, weep!
That the mountains tumbled, I wept,
That the sea rose up in dust, I lamented,
Wailing that he, my lord, had gone.
In the Red Land, alas! thou art awaited
And there thou art bidden to sleep!
O only weep, weep!
Thou hast already set forth, my lord Ihuitimalli,
Xicalango-Zacanco has passed to thy command.
Alas and nevermore! Weep, weep!
Thy house will remain forever, thy palace
Carried across the sea will always stay.
Thou hast left Tollan of the boundaries
Desolate here, weep, ah, weep!
Without ceasing that lord, that Timallo wept:
Thy house will remain forever.
Thou first didst paint the stone and wood in Tollan,

> There where thou camest to rule, Nacxitl our noble lord!
> Never will thy name be forgotten,
> Always will thy people mourn thee, bewail thee!
> The Turquoise House, the Serpent House
> Thou alone didst set it up in Tollan,
> There where thou camest to rule, Nacxitl our noble lord!

The Aztec poems which have been translated comprise hymns, war songs, chronicles, laments, prophecies, lyrics of praise, and reflective verse of a very high order.

The best American Indian hymns to native gods are to be found in Brinton's *Rig Veda Americanus*. Twenty of these highly poetic chants are there given, translated from the Nahuatl language as it had been transliterated into the Spanish alphabet in the original manuscript of Father Bernardino de Sahagun, one of the earliest Mexican missionaries. Three of these hymns will here be offered.

These verses are colored throughout by a yearning for earthly consolation and by a sophisticated melancholy, two traits evident in poem after poem found in the surviving literature of the Aztecs. The triumph of these northern barbarians over the Toltec and other Nahua groups in the Valley of Mexico had been achieved solely by a ferocious energy in war, and even after a century of contact with the cultures of the vanquished, the highest worship of the Aztecs was reserved for the gruesome deity Huitzilopochtli, god of war and bloodshed, who delighted in the smoking heart of the sacrificial victim and whose rites horrified even the veterans of Cortés. War was the grand ritual; and when the enemy was subdued, sham battles and gladiatorial combats were celebrated. The never wholly civilized minds of the Aztecs suffered a curious involution; the race became decadent before it could become ripe; and the adoption of the arts and sciences they found in southern Mexico laid only a superficial varnish upon the grim mask of the warrior. The result may be found in the sculptural figures they used to adorn their temples—intricate traceries of serpent heads, necklaces of skulls, grotesque symbols of death in its most revolting forms. Most of their poems reveal an equally intricate technical ingenuity applied with a savage preoccupation with morbid subject-matter.

The first hymn to be given is dedicated to Tlaloc, an important deity who controlled the waters, the rains, the thunder and lightning. The annual festival in his honor was held at the time of corn-planting, when his beneficence was invoked. "Tlalocan," the place of Tlaloc, was equivalent to the earthly paradise; and the reference in the ninth stanza seems, says Brinton, to apply to the belief that the souls of the departed warriors passed from earth for four years and then returned to the terrestrial paradise of Tlaloc.

HYMN TO TLALOC [29]

In Mexico the god appears; thy banner is unfolded in all directions, and no one weeps.

I, the god, have returned again.
I have turned again to the place of abundance of blood-sacrifices; there when the day grows old, I am beheld as a god.

Thy work is that of a noble magician; truly thou hast made thyself to be of our flesh; thou hast made thyself, and who dare affront thee?

Truly he who affronts me does not find himself well with me; my fathers took by the head the tigers and the serpents.

In Tlalocan, in the verdant house, they play at ball, they cast the reeds.

Go forth, go forth to where the clouds are spread abundantly, where the thick mist makes the cloudy house of Tlaloc.

There with strong voice I rise up and cry aloud.

Go ye forth to seek me, seek for the words which I have said, as I rise, a terrible one, and cry aloud.

After four years they shall go forth, not to be known, not to be numbered, they shall descend to the beautiful house, to unite together and know the doctrine.

Go forth, go forth to where the clouds are spread abundantly, where the thick mist makes the cloudy home of Tlaloc.

The second example is a song of fasting invoking several divinities, such as Tonan, "Our Mother"; Tlazolteotl, goddess of carnal love; Cinteotl, god of maize and fertility; and Quetzalcoatl, the famous "Plumed Serpent," exiled ruler of Tollan. The flowers mentioned are the youths and maidens who die young; and the "house of the ball player" is the tomb.

HYMN OF FASTING [29]

The flower in my heart blossoms and spreads abroad in the middle of the night.

Tonan has satisfied her passion, the goddess Tlazolteotl has satisfied her passion.

I, Cinteotl, was born in Paradise, I come from the place of flowers. I am the only flower, the new, the glorious one.

Cinteotl was born from the water; he came born as a mortal, as a youth, from the cerulean home of the fishes, a new, a glorious god.

He shone forth as the sun; his mother dwelt in the house of the dawn, varied in hue as the *quechol* bird, a new, a glorious flower.

I came forth on the earth, even to the market place like a mortal, even I, Quetzalcoatl, great and glorious.

Be ye happy under the flower-bush varied in hue as a quetzal bird; listen to the *quechol* singing to the gods; listen to the singing of the *quechol* along the river; hear its flute along the river in the house of the reeds.

Alas! would that my flowers would cease from dying; our flesh is as flowers, even as flowers in the place of flowers.

He plays at ball, he plays at ball, the servant of marvelous skill; he plays at ball, the precious servant; look at him; even the ruler of the nobles follows him to his house.

O youths! O youths! follow the example of your ancestors; make yourselves equal to them in the ball court; establish ourselves in your houses.

She goes to the mart, they carry Xochiquetzal to the mart; she speaks at Cholula; she startles my heart; she startles my heart; she has not finished, the priest knows her; where the merchants sell green jade earrings she is to be seen, in the place of wonders she is to be seen.

Sleep, sleep, sleep, O fold my hands to sleep, I, O woman, sleep.

The third hymn is more suggestive of the sanguinary side of the Aztec religion. Xipe Totec, "Lord of the Flayed," was, according to Brinton, "the patron divinity of the silversmiths, and his festival, attended with peculiarly bloody rites, was celebrated in the first month of the calendar. . . . His high priest was called Youallauan, 'the nocturnal tippler,' . . . and it was his duty to tear out the hearts of the human victims." [29]

HYMN OF THE HIGH PRIEST OF XIPE TOTEC [29]

The nightly drinking, why should I oppose it?
Go forth and array yourselves in the golden garments, clothe your-selves in the glittering vestments.

My god descended upon the water, into the beautiful glistening surface; he was as a lovely water cypress, as a beauteous green serpent; now I have left behind me my suffering.

I go forth, I go forth about to destroy, I, Yoatzin; my soul is in the cerulean water; I am seen in the golden water; I shall appear unto mortals; I shall strengthen them for the words of war!

My god appears as a mortal; O Yoatzin, thou art seen upon the mountains; I shall appear unto mortals; I shall strengthen them for the words of war.

War was not only a means of conquest but a divine sport to the Nahuatl city-builders of Mexico. A number of Aztec poems glorify-ing war are given by Brinton, from whose translations two have here been chosen. The first of these is supposed to have been sung by the poet to persuade certain friends to turn their minds toward the beauties of battle. He pointed out that life is brief, that the dead do not return to the joys of earth, and that the greatest of these joys is to be found on the field of combat.

A WAR SONG OF THE OTOMIES [26]

It grieves me, dear friends, that you walk not with me in spirit, that
    I have not your company in the scenes of joy and pleasure, that
    never more in union do we seek the same paths.

Do you really see me, dear friends?
Will no god take the blindness from your eyes?
What is life on earth?
Can the dead return?
No, they live far within the heavens, in a place of joy.

The joy of the Lord, the Giver of Life, is where the warriors sing,
    and the smoke of the war-fire rises up; where the flowers of the
    shields spread abroad their leaves; where deeds of valor shake
    the earth; where the fatal flowers of death cover the fields.

The battle is there, the beginning of the battle is there, in the open
    fields, where the smoke of the war-fire winds around and curls
    upward from the fatal war-flowers which adorn you, ye friends
    and warriors of the Chichimecs.

Let not my soul dread that open field; I earnestly desire the begin-
    ning of the slaughter, my soul longs for the murderous fray.

The war-cloud rises upward, it rises into the blue sky where dwells
    the Giver of Life; in it blossom forth the flowers of prowess
    and valor; beneath it, in the battlefield, the children ripen to
    maturity.

Rejoice with me, dear friends, and do ye rejoice, ye children, going
    forth to the open field of battle; let us rejoice and revel amid
    these shields, flowers of the murderous fray.

The second of these war songs was composed by an Aztec prince
of the historical period, Tetlapan Quetzanitzin, who at the time of
the entrance of Cortés into the Mexican metropolis was ruler of
Tlacopan or Tacuba, one of its suburbs on the mainland of Lake
Texcoco. When the Spanish leader demanded the imprisonment of
the Emperor Montezuma as a hostage and kidnaped the monarch in
the midst of his own city, Tetlapan was one of the attendants of
Montezuma, and it is recorded that he made his escape and later

joined the party of Quahtemoctzin, Montezuma's tragic young heir.

This song, highly metaphorical, seems at first to be a drinking song; yet the drunkenness is not that of the white pulque wine, but of the intoxicating draught of battle. The "shattered stones" are the young warriors slain on the field, and the dew is the blood of enemies. The flowers which the singer celebrates are the decorated war shields of the contesting heroes. Both this poem and the previous one may be taken to apply to the "flowery war," a curious custom of the ancient Mexicans of making war upon neighboring tribes not to settle any grievances or to annex new territory, but merely to display warlike skill and to take captives to swell the host of human sacrifices demanded by the temple rites. This custom has been mentioned in many places, and the rules relating to single combat and the penalties to the vanquished bear more than slight resemblance to the rules of knightly tourney in medieval Europe.

A WAR SONG OF TETLAPAN QUETZANITZIN [23]

Why did it grieve you, O friends, why did it pain you, that you were drunk with the wine?

Arise from your stupor, O friends, come hither and sing; let us seek for homes in some flowery land; forget your drunkenness.

The precept is old that one should quaff the strong white wine in the moment of difficulty, as when one enters the battle plain, when he goes forth to the place of shattered stones, where the precious stones are splintered, the emeralds, the turquoises, the youths, the children.

Therefore, friends and brothers, quaff now the flowing white wine.

Let us drink together amid the flowers, let us build our houses among the flowers, where the fragrant blossoms cast abroad their odors as a fountain its waters, where the breath of the dew-laden flowers makes sweet the air; there it is that nobility and strength will make glorious our houses, there the flowers of war bloom over a fertile land.

O friends, do you not hear me?

Let us go, let us go, let us pour forth the white wine, the strong wine of battle; let us drink the wine which is as sweet as the dew of roses, let it intoxicate our souls, let our souls be steeped in its delights, let them be enriched as in some opulent place, some fertile land.

Why does it trouble you?

Come with me, and listen to my song.

The traditional history of the Nahua tribes is recited in several poems from Brinton's *Ancient Nahuatl Poetry*, such as the lengthy "Reign of Tezozomoctli," which mentions Chicomoztoc or the "Seven Caves," legendary birthplace of the Aztecs, and the "Lament for Quetzalcoatl," mourning the downfall of the great Toltec chiefs.

A polished song of lamentation has been translated by Brinton from an Aztec composition "by a certain ruler in memory of former rulers." It was certainly written before the advent of the missionaries, and the tone is non-Christian in its gloomy and despairing abandonment of consolation. The "Cause of All" and the "Giver of Life" are not to be confused with any doctrine of Christian divinity, but represent some Aztec god of creation and destruction. The despairing cry of the poet is fully in keeping with the nature of a race whose mythology mentions no more comforting scene for the afterlife than a stony dark plain upon which falls a continual storm of obsidian arrowheads.

BY A CERTAIN RULER IN MEMORY OF FORMER RULERS [23]

Weeping, I, the singer, weave my song of flowers of sadness; I call to memory the youths, the shards, the fragments, gone to the land of the dead; once noble and powerful here on earth, the youths were dried up like feathers, were split into fragments like an emerald, before the face and in the sight of those who saw them on earth, and with the knowledge of the Cause of All.

Alas! alas! I sing in grief as I recall the children.

Would that I could turn back again; would that I could grasp their hands once more; would that I could call them forth from the land of the dead; would that we could bring them again on earth, that they might rejoice and we rejoice, and that they might rejoice and delight the Giver of Life; is it possible that we his servants should reject him or should be ungrateful?

Thus I weep in my heart as I, the singer, review my memories, recalling things sad and grievous.

Would only that I knew they could hear me, there in the land of
the dead, were I to sing some worthy song.
Would that I could gladden them, that I could console the suffering
and the torment of the children.
How can it be learned?
Whence can I draw the inspiration?
They are not where I may follow them; neither can I reach them
with my calling as one here on earth.

The conquest of the Aztecs in 1521 by the Spanish adventurers led
by Cortés was foretold by many omens and dire prophecies during
the preceding years. These are mentioned by a number of writers,
and it is quite possible that the conquest was made easier by the
fatalistic attitude of the people, led by their superstitious and gloomy
priest-king. Among these omens was a comet which during the entire
year 1509 was visible after midnight. This is the "smoking star"
mentioned in the poem below, and from its appearance the singer
inferred that the existence of the Aztecs as a nation was doomed.

PROPHECY OF DESTRUCTION [23]

The sweet voiced *quechol* there, ruling the earth, has intoxicated my
soul.

I am like the quetzal bird, I am created in the house of the one
only God; I sing sweet songs among the flowers; I chant songs
and rejoice in my heart.

The fuming dewdrops from the flowers in the field intoxicate my
soul.

I grieve to myself that ever this dwelling on earth should end.

I foresaw, being a Mexican, that our rule began to be destroyed;
I went forth weeping that it was to bow down and be destroyed.

Let me not be angry that the grandeur of Mexico is to be destroyed.

The smoking stars gather together against it; the one who cares for
flowers is about to be destroyed.

He who cared for books wept, he wept for the beginning of the
destruction.

There is a paucity of good secular poetry of the lyric sort in the translations of American Indian verse, in comparison with the abundance to be found in poetry of the European tradition. This may be explained by the fact that the Indian is essentially non-individualistic, but rather is community-minded. The romantic or egotistical exhibition of his personal impressions of the world was foreign to his nature, and such an act would have been looked upon by his fellow tribesmen not only as impractical, but as dangerously anti-social. Except among the Aztec tribe, Indian life offered no public occasions upon which a poet would be invited to express his inmost lyrical thoughts in verse of his own composition.

Two lyrics translated by Brinton consciously celebrate the art of poetry. The first of these "has every inherent mark of antiquity, and its thought is free from any tincture of European influence."

AN OTOMI SONG OF THE MEXICANS [23]

I, the singer, polished my noble new song like a shining emerald, I arranged it like the voice of the *tzinitzcan* bird, I called to mind the essence of poetry, I set it in order like the chant of the *zacuan* bird, I mingled it with the beauty of the emerald, that I might make it appear like a rose bursting its bud, so that I might rejoice the Cause of All.

I skillfully arranged my song like the lovely feathers of the *zacuan* bird, the *tzinitzcan* and the *quechol;* I shall speak forth my song like the tinkling of golden bells; my song is that which the *miaua* bird pours forth around him; I lifted my voice and rained down flowers of speech before the face of the Cause of All.

In the true spirit of song I lifted my voice through a trumpet of gold, I let fall from my lips a celestial song, I shall speak notes precious and brilliant as those of the *miaua* bird, I shall cause to blossom out a noble new song, I lifted my voice like the burning incense of flowers, so that I the singer might cause joy before the face of the Cause of All.

The divine *quechol* bird answers me as I, the singer, sing, like the *coyol* bird, a noble new song, polished like a jewel, a turquoise, a shining emerald, darting green rays, a flower song of spring, spreading a celestial fragrance, fresh with the dews of roses, thus have I the poet sung.

I colored with skill, I mingled choice roses in a noble new song, polished like a jewel, a turquoise, a shining emerald, darting green rays, a flower song of spring, spreading celestial fragrance, fresh with the dews of roses, thus have I the poet sung.

I was glorified, I was enriched, by the flower-sweet song as by the smoke of the *poyomatl*, my soul was contented, I trembled in spirit, I inhaled the sweetness, my soul was intoxicated, I inhaled the fragrance of delicious flowers in the place of riches, my soul was drunken with the flowers.

Another Aztec poem in which the singer celebrates his art—and indirectly praises the grandeur of Montezuma, from whom he seeks aid in war—is interesting. "The occurrence to which this poem alludes," says Brinton, "took place about the year 1507. The chroniclers state that it was in the early period of the reign of Montezuma II, that the natives of Huezotzinco, at that time allies of the Mexicans, were severely harassed by the Tlascallans, and applied, not in vain, to their powerful suzerain to aid them. . . . The song would appear to be used as a delicate prelude to the more serious negotiations. From the references in verses one and three we infer that this singer held in his hand the painted book from which he recited the couplets." [23]

A SONG OF THE HUEZOTZINCOS [23]

Raining down writings for thy mind, O Montezuma, I come hither, I come raining them down, a very jester, a painted butterfly; stringing together pretty objects, I seem to be as one cementing together precious stones, as I chant my song on my emerald flute, as I blow on my golden flute, *ya ho, ay la.*

Yes, I shall cause thy flowers to rejoice the Giver of Life, the God in heaven, as hither I come raining down my songs, *ya ho.*

A sweet-voiced flower is my mind, a sweet-voiced flower is my drum, and I sing the words of this flowery book.

Rejoice and be glad ye who live amid the flowers in the house of my great lord Montezuma, we must finish with this earth, we must finish with the sweet flowers, alas.

At the Mount of Battle we bring forth our sweet and glittering flowers before God, plants having the luster of the tiger, like the cry of the eagle, leaving glorious memory, such are the plants of this house.

Alas! in a little while there is an end before God to all living; let me therefore string together beauteous and yellow feathers, and mingling them with the dancing butterflies rain them down before you, scattering the words of my song like water dashed from flowers.

I would that I could go there where lies the great blue water surging, and smoking and thundering, till after a time it retires again: I shall sing as the quetzal, the blue *quechol*, when I go back to Huezotzinco among the waters.

I shall follow them, I shall know them, my beloved Huezotzincos; the emerald *quechol* birds, the green *quechol*, the golden butterflies, and yellow birds, guard Huezotzinco among the waters.

Among the flowery waters, the golden waters, the emerald waters, at the junction of the waters which the blue duck rules, moving her spangled tail.

I the singer stand on high on the yellow rushes; let me go forth with noble songs and laden with flowers.

Another lyric is the lament of a Huezotzinco prisoner held captive in Tlatilolco, a suburb of the Aztec capital, whose song is filled with hatred for his captors and a thirst for vengeance upon them. Brinton dates the composition as not later than 1511.

A SONG OF HUEZOTZINCO [23]

Only sad flowers, sad songs, are here in Mexico, in Tlatilolco, in this place these alone are known, alas.

It is well to know these, if only we may please the Giver of Life, lest we be destroyed, we his subjects, alas.

We have angered him, we are only wretched beings, slaves, by flood; we have seen and known affliction, alas.

We are disturbed, we are embittered, thy servants here in Tlatilolco, deprived of food, made acquainted with affliction, we are fatigued by labor, O Giver of Life, alas.

Weeping is with us, tears fall like rain, here in Tlatilolco; as the Mexican women go down to the water, we beg of them for ourselves and our friends, alas.

Even as the smoke, rising, lies in a cloud over Mount Atloyan, in Mexico, so does it happen unto us, O Giver of Life, alas.

And you Mexicans, may you remember concerning us when you descend and suffer before the majesty of God, when there you shall howl like wolves.

There, there will be only weeping as your greeting when you come, there you will be accursed, all of you, workers in filth, slaves, rulers or warriors, and thus Tenochtitlan will be deserted.

O friends, do not weep, but know that sometime we shall have left behind us the things of Mexico, and then their water shall be made bitter and their food shall be made bitter, here in Tlatilolco, as never before, by the Giver of Life.

The disdained and the slaves shall go forth with song; but in a little while their oppressors shall be seen in the fire, amid the howling of wolves.

The most important poet among the Nahuatl tribes of Mexico was Nezahualcoyotl, ruler of Texcoco, who died in 1472 at the age of eighty. During the early part of his life, this heir to one of the most beautiful of the old lakeside cities of Anáhuac was kept from his rightful place by an usurper. Much of this time he was in poverty and a fugitive from King Tezozomoc, who had murdered the young man's father; and the name of Nezahualcoyotl, meaning "hungry wolf," commemorates these days of fasting and daring persistence in seeking to regain his heritage. When he came at last to rule, he acted as a great patron of the arts, poetry in particular. Not only did he seek out and entertain the best native bards, but he himself is credited with the composition of sixty chants.

Several verses by this noble poet have been translated into English by Smisor from the Spanish manuscript of Garibay and checked with the original Nahuatl. Here is a brief example:

LIFE OF ILLUSION [181]

Is it true that one lives on earth?
Perhaps forever on earth? Only a brief instant here!
Until the fine stones split asunder,
Until gold breaks to pieces, until precious feathers disintegrate,
Perhaps forever on earth? Only a brief instant here!

Four songs attributed to Nezahualcoyotl have survived complete and were translated by Brinton. All these fine poems are expressive of a philosophic view of life more elevated than anything else that remains to us from the pre-Conquest period of Indian history. The one now to be presented—which was given in a different version by Prescott in the appendix to his *Conquest of Mexico* more than a century ago—was said to have been composed by the king at the time he dedicated his palace. Its sincere and dignified pondering upon the mystery of mortality, and its restatement of the *ubi sunt* theme among the "unenlightened" denizens of the New World, is heightened by a groping apprehension of a divine creator, and tinged with the decadent tone of Aztec poems previously presented. A fitting conclusion to this volume on North American Indian poetry is the offering of this unique example of an aboriginal "Thanatopsis."

SONG OF NEZAHUALCOYOTL [23]

The fleeting pomps of the world are like the green willow trees, which, aspiring to permanence, are consumed by a fire, fall before the ax, are upturned by the wind, or are scarred and saddened by age.

The grandeurs of life are like the flowers in color and in fate; the beauty of these remains so long as their chaste buds gather and store the rich pearls of the dawn and saving it, drop it in liquid dew; but scarcely has the Cause of All directed upon them the full rays of the sun, when their beauty and glory fail, and the brilliant gay colors which decked forth their pride wither and fade.

The delicious realms of flowers count their dynasties by short periods; those which in the morning revel proudly in beauty and strength, by evening weep for the sad destruction of their thrones, and for the mishaps which drive them to loss, to poverty, to death and to the grave.

All things of earth have an end, and in the midst of the most joyous lives, the breath falters, they fall, they sink into the ground.

All the earth is a grave, and naught escapes it; nothing is so perfect that it does not fall and disappear.

The rivers, brooks, fountains and waters flow on, and never return to their joyous beginnings; they hasten on to the vast realms of Tlaloc, and the wider they spread between their marges the more rapidly do they mold their own sepulchral urns.

That which was yesterday is not today; and let not that which is today trust to live tomorrow.

The caverns of the earth are filled with pestilential dust which once was the bones, the flesh, the bodies of great ones who sate upon thrones, deciding causes, ruling assemblies, governing armies, conquering provinces, possessing treasures, tearing down temples, flattering themselves with pride, majesty, fortune, praise and dominion.

These glories have passed like the dark smoke thrown out by the fires of Popocatepetl, leaving no monuments but the rude skins on which they are written.

Ha! ha! Were I to introduce you into the obscure bowels of this temple, and were to ask you which of these bones were those of the powerful Achalchiuhtlanextin, first chief of the ancient Toltecs; of Necazecmitl, devout worshiper of the gods; if I inquire where is the peerless beauty of the glorious empress Xiuhtzal, where the peaceable Topiltzin, last monarch of the hapless land of Tulan; if I ask you where are the sacred ashes of our first father Xolotl; those of the bounteous Nopal; those of the generous Tlotzin; or even the still warm cinders of my glorious and immortal, though unhappy and luckless father Ixtlilxochitl; if I continued thus questioning about all our august ancestors, what would you reply?

The same that I reply—I know not, I know not; for first and last are confounded in the common clay.

What was their fate shall be ours, and of all who follow us.

Unconquered princes, warlike chieftains, let us seek, let us sigh for
the heaven, for there all is eternal, and nothing is corruptible.

The darkness of the sepulchre is but the strengthening couch for
the glorious sun, and the obscurity of the night but serves to
reveal the brilliancy of the stars.

No one has power to alter these heavenly lights, for they serve to
display the greatness of their Creator, and as our eyes see them
now, so saw them our earliest ancestors, and so shall see them our
latest posterity.

BIBLIOGRAPHY

BIBLIOGRAPHY ON NORTH AMERICAN INDIAN POETRY

1. ALEXANDER, HARTLEY BURR. Indian Songs and English Verse. *American Speech*, vol. 1, August, 1926, pp. 571–575.
2. —— Latin America. *The Mythology of All Races*, vol. 11, Boston, 1920. ix + 424 pp.
3. —— North America. *Ibid.*, vol. 10. xxiv + 325 pp.
4. AUSTIN, MARY (HUNTER). *The American Rhythm*. New York, 1923. viii + 155 pp.
5. —— Imagism: Original and Aboriginal. *Dial*, vol. 67, August 23, 1919, pp. 162–163.
6. —— Non-English Writings: II, Aboriginal. In *Cambridge History of American Literature*, vol. 4, pp. 610–634.
7. —— The Path on the Rainbow. *Dial*, vol. 66, May 31, 1919, pp. 569–570.
8. BAILEY, VIRGINIA. Indian Music of the Southwest. *El Palacio*, vol. 44, 1938, pp. 1–3.
9. BAKER, THEODOR. *Ueber die Musik der Nordamerikanischen Wilden*. Leipzig, Germany, 1882. 82 pp.
10. BARBEAU, M. Asiatic Survivals in Indian Songs. *Scientific Monthly*, vol. 54, April, 1942, pp. 303–307.
11. BARNES, NELLIE. *American Indian Love Lyrics and Other Verse*. Foreword by Mary Austin. New York, 1925. 190 pp.
12. —— American Indian Verse, Characteristics of Style. *Bulletin* of University of Kansas, vol. 22, no. 18. Lawrence, Kans., 1921. 63 pp.
13. BEAUCHAMP, WILLIAM M. Civil, Religious and Mourning Councils and Ceremonies of Adoption of the New York Indians. New York State Museum *Bulletin 113*, June, 1907, pp. 337–451.
14. —— Wampum and Shell Articles Used by the New York Indians. *Ibid.*, *Bulletin 8*, February, 1901, pp. 321–480.
15. BIMBONI, A. *Songs of the American Indians*, New York, 1917. BOAS, FRANZ. See RINK.
16. BOAS, FRANZ. The Central Eskimo. *6th Annual Report*, Bureau of American Ethnology, Washington, D. C., 1888, pp. 399–669.
17. —— Chinook Songs. *Journal of American Folk-Lore*, vol. 1, 1888, pp. 220–226.

18. [SAME] Eskimo Tales and Songs. *Ibid.*, vol. 7, 1894, pp. 45–50.
19. —— Ethnology of the Kwakiutl. *35th Annual Report*, Bureau of American Ethnology, Washington, D. C., 1921; part 1, pp. 41–794; part 2, pp. 795–1481.
20. —— *Religion of the Kwakiutl Indians.* Columbia Univ. Contributions to Anthropology. New York, 1930. 2 vol.
21. —— Stylistic Aspects of Primitive Literature. *Journal of American Folk-Lore*, vol. 38, 1925, pp. 329–339.
22. BRINTON, DANIEL G. *Aboriginal American Authors.* Philadelphia, 1883. viii + 63 pp.
23. —— *Ancient Nahuatl Poetry.* Library of American Aboriginal Literature, vol. 7. Philadelphia, 1887. viii + 177 pp.
24. ——*The Annals of the Cakchiquels.* Library of American Aboriginal Literature, vol. 6. Philadelphia, 1885. vii + 234 pp.
25. —— *The Comedy-Ballet of Güegüence.* Library of American Aboriginal Literature, vol. 3. Philadelphia, 1883. 146 pp.
26. —— *Essays of an Americanist.* Philadelphia, 1890. xii + 469 pp. *exposes spurious poem (see pp 17-18 here)*
27. —— *The Lênapé and Their Legends.* Library of American Aboriginal Literature, vol. 5. Philadelphia, 1885. 262 pp.
28. —— *The Maya Chronicles.* Library of American Aboriginal Literature, vol. 1. Philadelphia, 1882. vii + 279 pp.
29. —— *Rig Veda Americanus; Sacred Songs of the Ancient Mexicans.* Library of American Aboriginal Literature, vol. 8. Philadelphia, 1890. iv + 95 pp.
30. BUNZEL, RUTH L. Introduction to Zuñi Ceremonialism. *47th Annual Report*, Bureau of American Ethnology, Washington, D. C., 1932, pp. 469–544.
31. —— Zuñi Katzinas. *Ibid.*, pp. 837–1086.
32. —— Zuñi Ritual Poetry. *Ibid.*, pp. 613–835.
BURLIN. See CURTIS.
33. BURTON, FREDERICK R. *American Primitive Music with Especial Attention to the Songs of the Ojibways.* New York, 1909. 283 pp.
34. BUTTREE, JULIA M. *The Rhythm of the Redman.* New York, 1930. xv + 280 pp.
CAMPBELL, W. S. See VESTAL, STANLEY.
35. CAMPOS, RUBÉN M. *La Producción Literaria de los Aztecas.* Secretaría de Educación Pública, Mexico, D. F. No date. 464 pp.

36. CHAMBERLIN, ALEXANDER F. Primitive Woman as Poet. *Journal of American Folk-Lore*, vol. 16, 1903, pp. 207–221.

37. CONVERSE, HARRIET M. (edited by ARTHUR C. PARKER) Myths and Legends of the New York State Iroquois. New York State Museum *Bulletin 125*, December 15, 1908. 196 pp.

38. CORNYN, JOHN HUBERT. Ancient Aztec Poem. *Mexican Folkways*, vol. 2, 1926, pp. 20–22.

39. ——— Song to the Wind God. *World Review*, vol. 7, October 15, 1928, p. 73.

40. CRINGAN, ALEX T. Pagan Dance Songs of the Iroquois. Archaeological Report, 1899, being part of appendix to Report of Minister of Education, Ontario. Toronto, 1900.

41. CRONYN, GEORGE. Indian Melodists and Mr. Untermeyer. *Dial*, vol. 67, August 23, 1919, p. 162.

42. ——— *The Path on the Rainbow*. Introduction by Mary Austin. New York, 1918 and 1934. xxxii + 360 pp. *see #26* Ep 32 here

43. CURTIN, JEREMIAH. *Creation Myths of Primitive America*. Boston, 1898. xxxix + 530 pp.

44. CURTIS (BURLIN), NATALIE. *The Indians' Book*. New York, 1907 and 1923. 582 pp.

45. CUSHING, FRANK HAMILTON. Outlines of Zuñi Creation Myths. *13th Annual Report*, Bureau of American Ethnology, Washington, D. C., 1896, pp. 321–447.

46. ——— *Zuñi Breadstuff*. New York, 1920. 673 pp.

47. DAUGHERTY, GEORGE H. American Indian Compositions Reflecting the Social and Political Organization of the Tribes. *Open Court*, vol. 41, 1927, pp. 80–89.

48. ——— Differentiation of Indian Cultures According to Geographical Areas. *Ibid.*, pp. 288–305.

49. ——— Motives of Indian Speeches and Songs. *Open Court*, vol. 40, 1926, pp. 689–704, 719–733.

50. ——— Songs and Speeches of the Plains. *Ibid.*, 1927, pp. 338–357.

51. ——— Technique of Indian Composition. *Open Court*, vol. 41, 1927, pp. 150–166.

52. DAY, A. GROVE. Types of North American Indian Poetry in English Translation. Ph.D. Dissertation, Stanford University, 1943. 263 pp.

53. DE HUFF, ELIZABETH W. and GRUNN, HOMER. *From Desert and*

Pueblo: five authentic Navajo and Tewa Indian songs. Boston, 1924.

54. DENSMORE, FRANCES. *The American Indians and Their Music*. New York, 1926. 139 pp.

55. ———— *Cheyenne and Arapaho Music*. Southwest Museum Papers, no. 10, Los Angeles, May, 1936. 111 pp.

56. ———— Chippewa Music. *Bulletin 45*, Bureau of American Ethnology, Washington, D. C., 1910. xix + 216 pp.

57. ———— Chippewa Music II. *Bulletin 53*, Bureau of American Ethnology, Washington, D. C., 1913. xxi + 341 pp.

58. ———— Choctaw Music. *Bulletin 136*, Bureau of American Ethnology, Washington, D. C., 1943, pp. 101–188.

59. ———— Geronimo's Song. *Indian School Journal*, April, 1906.

60. ———— The Importance of Recordings of Indian Songs. *American Anthropologist*, vol. 47, 1945, pp. 637–639.

61. ———— *Indian Action Songs*. Boston, 1922. 12 pp.

62. ———— Mandan and Hidatsa Music. *Bulletin 80*, Bureau of American Ethnology, Washington, D. C., 1923. xx + 192 pp.

63. ———— Menominee Music. *Bulletin 102*, Bureau of American Ethnology, Washington, D. C., 1932. xxii + 230 pp.

64. ———— Music in Its Relation to the Religious Thought of the Teton Sioux. *Holmes Anniversary Volume*, Washington, D. C., 1916, pp. 67–79.

65. ———— Music of the Indians of British Columbia. *Bulletin 136*, Bureau of American Ethnology, Washington, D. C., 1943, pp. 1–99.

66. ———— *Music of Santo Domingo Pueblo, New Mexico*. Southwest Museum Papers, no. 12, May, 1938. 186 pp.

67. ———— *Music of the Tule Indians of Panama*. Smithsonian Miscellaneous Collections 77, no. 11, publ. 2864, Washington, D. C., 1926. 39 pp.

68. ———— Native Songs of Two Hybrid Ceremonies among the American Indians. *American Anthropologist*, vol. 43, January, 1941, pp. 78–82.

69. ———— Nootka and Quileute Music. *Bulletin 124*, Bureau of American Ethnology, Washington, D. C., 1939. xxvi + 358 pp.

70. ———— Northern Ute Music. *Bulletin 75*, Bureau of American Ethnology, Washington, D. C., 1922. 213 pp.

71. [SAME] Origin of a Siwash Song. *American Anthropologist*, vol. 47, January, 1945, pp. 173–175.

72. —— Papago Music. *Bulletin 90*, Bureau of American Ethnology, Washington, D. C., 1929. xx + 229 pp.

73. —— Pawnee Music. *Bulletin 93*, Bureau of American Ethnology, Washington, D. C., 1929. xviii + 129 pp.

74. —— *Poems from Sioux and Chippewa Songs*. Washington, D. C., 1917. 23 pp.

75. —— A Resemblance Between Yuman and Pueblo Songs. *American Anthropologist*, vol. 34, October, 1932, pp. 694–700.

76. —— A Search for Songs among the Chitimacha Indians of Louisiana. *Bulletin 133*, Bureau of American Ethnology, Washington, D. C., 1943, pp. 1–15.

77. —— Songs of the Indians. *American Mercury*, vol. 7, 1926, pp. 65–68.

78. —— The Study of Indian Music in the Nineteenth Century. *American Anthropologist*, vol. 29, 1927, pp. 77–86.

79. —— Survival of Omaha Songs. *American Anthropologist*, vol. 46, July, 1944, pp. 418–420.

80. —— Teton Sioux Music. *Bulletin 61*, Bureau of American Ethnology, Washington, D. C., 1918. xxviii + 561 pp.

81. —— Use of Meaningless Syllables in Indian Songs. *American Anthropologist*, vol. 45, January, 1943, pp. 160–162.

82. —— Yuman and Yaqui Music. *Bulletin 110*, Bureau of American Ethnology, Washington, D. C., 1932. xviii + 216 pp.

DORSEY, GEORGE A. See VOTH.

83. DORSEY, J. OWEN. Omaha Songs: II. *Journal of American Folk-Lore*, vol. 1, 1888, pp. 209–214.

84. —— Osage Traditions. *6th Annual Report*, Bureau of American Ethnology, Washington, D. C., 1888, pp. 375–397.

85. —— Ponka and Omaha Songs. *Journal of American Folk-Lore*, vol. 1, 1888, p. 65 and p. 209; vol. 2, 1889, pp. 271–276.

86. —— Songs of the He¢ucka Society. *Journal of American Folk-Lore*, vol. 1, 1888, pp. 65–68.

87. ESPINOSA, AURELIO M. Miscellaneous Materials from the Pueblo Indians of New Mexico. *Philological Quarterly*, vol. 21, no. 1, January, 1942, pp. 121–127.

88. FARLEY, FRANK E. The Dying Indian. *Kittridge Anniversary Papers*, Boston, 1913, pp. 251–260.

89. FEWKES, J. WALTER. A Contribution to Passamaquoddy Folk-Lore. *Journal of American Folk-Lore*, vol. 3, 1890, pp. 257–280.

90. FLETCHER, ALICE CUNNINGHAM. The Hako: A Pawnee Ceremony. *22nd Annual Report*, Bureau of American Ethnology, part 2, Washington, D. C., 1904, pp. 13–372.

91. ———— *Indian Games and Dances with Native Songs*. Boston, 1915. 139 pp.

92. ———— Indian Songs. *Century Magazine*, vol. 47, January, 1894, pp. 421–431.

93. ———— Indian Songs and Music. *Journal of American Folk-Lore*, vol. 11, 1898, pp. 85–105.

94. ———— *Indian Story and Song from North America*. Boston, 1900. 126 pp.

95. ———— The Omaha Tribe. *27th Annual Report*, Bureau of American Ethnology, Washington, D. C., 1911, pp. 15–654 (with Francis La Flesche).

96. ———— The Study of Indian Music. *Proceedings* of National Academy of Science, vol. 1, 1915, pp. 231–235.

97. ———— A Study of Omaha Indian Music. *Archaeological and Ethnological Papers*, Peabody Museum, Harvard University, vol. 1, no. 5, Cambridge, Mass., 1893, pp. 7–152.

98. ———— The Wawan or Pipe Dances of the Omahas. *17th and 18th Annual Reports*, Peabody Museum, Harvard University, Cambridge, Mass., 1884, pp. 308–344.

99. FORD, CLELLAN S. *Smoke from Their Fires*. New Haven, 1941. 248 pp.

100. GATSCHET, ALBERT SAMUEL. The Klamath Indians. *Contributions to North American Ethnology*, vol. 2, part 1, Bureau of American Ethnology, Washington, D. C., 1890. xvi + 711 pp.

101. GÉNIN, A. Notes on the Dances, Music and Songs of the Ancient and Modern Mexicans. Smithsonian Institution, *Annual Report* of the Board of Regents, 1920. Washington, D. C., 1922, pp. 657–677.

102. GILMAN, BENJAMIN IVES. Hopi Songs. *Journal of American Ethnology and Archaeology*, vol. 5, 1908, pp. 1–235.

103. ———— Zuñi Melodies. *Journal of American Ethnology and Archaeology*, vol. 1, 1891, pp. 65–91.

104. GODDARD, PLINY EARLE. Gotal—A Mescalero Apache Cere-

mony. In *Putnam Anniversary Volume*, New York, 1909, pp. 385–394.

105. —— The Masked Dancers of the Apache. *Holmes Anniversary Volume*, Washington, 1916, pp. 132–136.

106. —— Myths and Tales from the San Carlos Apache. *Anthropological Papers*, American Museum of Natural History, New York, 1918, vol. 24, part 1. 86 pp.

107. —— Myths and Tales from the White Mountain Apache. *Ibid.*, part 2, pp. 87–140.

108. —— Myths, Prayers and Songs of the Navajo. University of California *Publications* on American Archaeology and Ethnology, vol. 5, 1907–1910, pp. 21–63.

109. GRINNELL, GEORGE BIRD. *The Cheyenne Indians*. 2 vol. New Haven, 1923. Appendix C, pp. 392–394.

110. —— Notes on Some Cheyenne Songs. *American Anthropologist* (N.S.), vol. 5, 1903, pp. 312–322.
GRUNN, HOMER. See DE HUFF.
HAEBERLIN, H. K. See ROBERTS.

111. HAGUE, E. Eskimo Songs. *Journal of American Folk-Lore*, vol. 28, 1915, pp. 96–98.

112. HAILE, BERARD. *Origin Legend of the Navaho Enemy Way*. Yale University *Publications* in Anthropology, no. 17. New Haven, 1938. 320 pp.

113. —— *Origin Legend of the Navaho Flintway:* text and translation. Chicago, 1943. xi + 319 pp.

114. HALE, HORATIO. *Iroquois Book of Rites*. Library of American Aboriginal Literature, vol. 2, Philadelphia, 1883. 222 pp.

115. HARRINGTON, JOHN P. A Yuma Account of Origins. *Journal of American Folk-Lore*, vol. 21, 1908, pp. 324–348.

116. HARRINGTON, JOHN P. and ROBERTS, HELEN. Picuris Children's Stories, with Texts and Songs. *43rd Annual Report*, Bureau of American Ethnology, Washington, D. C., 1928, pp. 289–447.

117. HERZOG, GEORGE. Plains Ghost Dance and Great Basin Music. *American Anthropologist*, vol. 37, no. 3, part 1, July–September, 1935, pp. 403–419.

118. —— *Research in Primitive and Folk Music in the United States*. American Council of Learned Societies, Bulletin 24, 1936. iv + 97 pp.

119. HEWITT, J. M. B. Requickening Address of the Iroquois Con-

dolence Council: ed. by W. N. Fenton. Washington Academy of Science *Journal*, vol. 46, March, 1944, pp. 65–79.

120. —— The Requickening Address of the League of the Iroquois. *Holmes Anniversary Volume*, Washington, 1916.

121. HODGE, FREDERICK WEBB (ed.). Handbook of the American Indians North of Mexico. 2 vol. *Bulletin 30*, Bureau of American Ethnology, Washington, D. C., 1907. Articles "Poetry," "Nith-Songs," etc.

122. HOFFMAN, WALTER JAMES. The Midéwiwin or Grand Medicine Society of the Ojibwa. *7th Annual Report*, Bureau of American Ethnology, Washington, D. C., 1891, pp. 143–300.

HOIJER, HARRY. See KLAH.

123. HUFFMAN, B. Lament of the Umatilla. *Oregon Historical Quarterly*, vol. 41, June, 1940, p. 146.

124. Indian Songs. *World Review*, vol. 5, November 21, 1927, p. 151.

125. JEANCON, JEAN A. *Indian Song Book*. Denver, 1924.

JENNESS, D. See ROBERTS.

126. KEISER, ALBERT. *The Indian in American Literature*. New York, 1933. vi + 312 pp.

127. KENNEDY, KATHARINE K. Zuñi Rituals. *Poetry*, vol. 50, August, 1937, pp. 254–257.

128. KINSEY, MABEL C. Ojibwa Song. *Journal of American Folk-Lore*, vol. 46, 1933, pp. 416–417.

129. KIRK, RUTH. Grandfather of the Gods. *New Mexico Magazine*, vol. 14, July, 1936, pp. 28–29, 43–44.

130. —— In Beauty It Is Finished. *New Mexico Magazine*, vol. 13, December, 1935, pp. 16–17.

131. KLAH, HASTEEN. *Navajo Creation Myth: The Story of the Emergence*. Recorded by MARY C. WHEELWRIGHT. 237 pp. Santa Fe, N. M., Museum of Navajo Ceremonial Art, 1942. Contains songs translated by DR. HARRY HOIJER and edited by DR. GEORGE HERZOG.

KLUCKHOHN, CLYDE. See WYMAN.

132. KLUCKHOHN, CLYDE. The Great Chants of the Navajo. *Theatre Arts Monthly*, vol. 17, August, 1933, pp. 639–645.

133. KLUCKHOHN, CLYDE and WYMAN, LELAND C. An Introduction to Navajo Chant Practice. *Memoirs* of American Anthropological Association, vol. 53, 1940. 204 pp.

134. KROEBER, A. L. Cultural and Natural Areas of Native North

America. University of California *Publications* in American Archaeology and Ethnology, vol. 38, 1939. xii + 242 pp., 28 maps.

LA FLESCHE, FRANCIS. See FLETCHER.

135. LA FLESCHE, FRANCIS. The Osage Tribe. Published in 4 parts.

    a. I: Rite of the Chiefs; Sayings of the Ancient Men. *36th Annual Report,* Bureau of American Ethnology, Washington, D. C., 1921, pp. 37–597.

    b. II: The Rite of Vigil. *39th Annual Report,* Bureau of American Ethnology, Washington, D. C., 1925, pp. 31–630.

    c. III: Two Versions of the Child-Naming Rite. *43rd Annual Report,* Bureau of American Ethnology, Washington, D. C., 1928, pp. 23–164.

    d. IV: Songs of the Wa-xó-be. *45th Annual Report,* Bureau of American Ethnology, Washington, D. C., 1930, pp. 523–833.

136. —— War Ceremony and Peace Ceremony of the Osage Indians. *Bulletin 101,* Bureau of American Ethnology, Washington, D. C., 1939. 280 pp.

137. LELAND, CHARLES GODFREY and PRINCE, JOHN DYNELEY. *Kuloskap the Master and Other Algonkin Poems.* New York, 1902. 370 pp.

138. LESSER, ALEXANDER. *The Pawnee Ghost Dance Hand Game.* New York, 1933. x + 337 pp.

139. MARRIOTT, ALICE. *The Ten Grandmothers.* Norman, Oklahoma, 1945. 306 pp.

140. MASON, ALDEN. The Papago Harvest Festival. *American Anthropologist,* vol. 22, no. 1, 1920, pp. 13–25.

141. MATTHEWS, WASHINGTON. The Mountain Chant, A Navaho Ceremony. *5th Annual Report,* Bureau of American Ethnology, Washington, D. C., 1887, pp. 379–467.

142. —— Navaho Gambling Songs. *American Anthropologist,* vol. 2, no. 1 (O.S.), 1889, pp. 1–20.

143. —— Navaho Legends. *Memoirs* of American Folk-Lore Society, vol. 5, 1897. viii + 299 pp.

144. —— Navaho Myths, Prayers and Songs, with texts and translations. Edited by P. E. Goddard. University of California *Publications* in American Archaeology and Ethnology, vol. 5, no. 2, Berkeley, 1907. 63 pp.

145. [SAME] The Night Chant. *Memoirs* of American Museum of Natural History, vol. 16, New York, 1902. 332 pp.

146. —— Songs of Sequence of the Navahos. *Journal of American Folk-Lore*, vol. 7, 1894, pp. 185–194.

147. MINDELEFF, COSMOS. Navaho Houses. *17th Annual Report*, Bureau of American Ethnology, 1895, pp. 475–514.

148. MONTGOMERY, GUY. A Method of Studying the Structure of Primitive Verse Applied to the Songs of the Teton-Sioux. University of California *Publications* in Modern Philology, no. 11, 1922, pp. 269–283.

149. MOONEY, JAMES. The Ghost-Dance Religion. *14th Annual Report*, Bureau of American Ethnology, part 2, Washington, D. C., 1896, pp. 641–1110.

150. —— The Sacred Formulas of the Cherokees. *7th Annual Report*, Bureau of American Ethnology, Washington, D. C., 1891, pp. 301–397.

151. —— The Swimmer Manuscript: Cherokee Sacred Formulas and Medicinal Prescriptions (edited by Frans M. Olbrechts). *Bulletin 99*, Bureau of American Ethnology, Washington, D. C., 1932. xvii + 319 pp.

152. Navajo Goat Song. *Masterkey*, vol. 8, 1934, p. 188.

153. Navajo Songs. *Nation*, vol. 110, April 17, 1920, p. 517.

154. OAKES, MAUD. *Where the Two Came to Their Father:* a Navaho war ceremonial, given by Jeff King. New York, 1944. 100 pp.

155. OPLER, MORRIS EDWARD. *An Apache Life-Way*. Chicago, 1941. xvii + 500 pp.

156. PARSONS, ELSIE CLEWS. *Pueblo Indian Religion*. 2 vol. Chicago, 1939.

157. PEARCE, THOMAS M. American Traditions and Our Histories of Literature. *American Literature*, vol. 14, November, 1942, pp. 277–284.

158. POUND, LOUISE. *Poetic Origins and the Ballad*, Chap. I. New York, 1921. x + 247 pp.

159. PRESCOTT, WILLIAM HICKLING. *History of the Conquest of Mexico*, 1843. Appendix contains translation of "Song of Nezahualcoyotl."

PRINCE, JOHN D. See LELAND.

160. RADIN, PAUL. *The Road of Life and Death:* a ritual drama of the American Indians. New York, 1945. ix + 345 pp.

161. —— The Winnebago Tribe. *37th Annual Report,* Bureau of American Ethnology, Washington, D. C., 1923, pp. 33–560.

162. READE, JOHN. Aboriginal American Poetry. *Transactions,* Royal Society of Canada, Ottawa, 1887, vol. 5, sec. 2, pp. 9–34.

163. —— Some Wabanaki Songs. *Ibid.,* pp. 1–8.

164. REAGAN, A. B. Medicine Songs of George Farmer. *American Anthropologist,* vol. 24, 1922, pp. 332–369.

165. REICHARD, GLADYS A. *Spider Woman: A Story of Navajo Weavers and Chanters.* New York, 1934. 287 pp.

166. RINK, HEINRICH and BOAS, FRANZ. Eskimo Tales and Songs. *Journal of American Folk-Lore,* vol. 2, 1889, pp. 123–131.

167. RINK, HEINRICH. *Tales and Traditions of the Eskimo.* London, 1875. 472 pp.

ROBERTS, HELEN H. See HARRINGTON.

168. ROBERTS, HELEN H. Chakwena Songs of Zuñi and Laguna. *Journal of American Folk-Lore,* vol. 36, 1923, pp. 177–184.

169. ROBERTS, HELEN H. and HAEBERLIN, H. K. Some Songs of the Puget Sound Salish. *Journal of American Folk-Lore,* vol. 31, 1918, pp. 496–520.

170. ROBERTS, HELEN H. and JENNESS, D. Songs of the Copper Eskimo. *Report* of the Canadian Arctic Expedition, 1913–1918, vol. 14. Ottawa, 1925. 506 pp.

171. ROYS, RALPH L. *The Book of Chilam Balam of Chumayel.* Carnegie Institution of Washington, 1933. viii + 229 pp.

172. RUSSELL, FRANK. The Pima Indians. *26th Annual Report,* Bureau of American Ethnology, Washington, D. C., 1908, pp. 3–389.

173. SAPIR, EDWARD. Song Recitative in Paiute Mythology. *Journal of American Folk-Lore,* vol. 23, 1910, pp. 455–472.

SAPIR, J. D. See SPECK.

174. SCHOOLCRAFT, HENRY ROWE. *Algic Researches.* New York, 1839.

175. —— *Historical and Statistical Information Respecting the History, Condition, and Prospects of the Indian Tribes of the United States.* 6 vol. Philadelphia, 1851–1857. Reissued under various titles; e.g., *Archives of Original Knowledge,* 1860.

176. —— *Oneóta:* or, The Red Race of America. New York,

1844–1845. 512 pp. Reissued under various titles: *The Red Race of America*, 1847; *The Indian in His Wigwam*, 1848; *The American Indians*, 1850; *Western Scenes and Reminiscences*, 1853.

177. SHOEMAKER, HENRY WHARTON. *Indian Folk-Songs of Pennsylvania*. Ardmore, Penna., 1927. 16 pp.

178. SISTRUNK, N. A. *Heart Poems of Silver Springs and Indian Legends of Florida*. Ocala, Fla., 1917. 56 pp.

179. SKINNER, A. Songs of the Menomini Medicine Ceremony. *American Anthropologist*, vol. 27, April, 1925, pp. 290–314.

180. SKINNER, CONSTANCE LINDSAY. Aztec Poets. *Poetry*, vol. 26, June, 1925, pp. 166–168.

181. SMISOR, G. T. Fifteen Short Aztec Poems. *Mexicana Review*, Winter, 1941, pp. 3–10.

182. SPECK, FRANK G. *Naskapi:* The savage hunters of the Labrador Peninsula. Norman, Oklahoma, 1935. 248 pp.

183. SPECK, FRANK G. with SAPIR, J. D. Ceremonial Songs of the Creek and Yuchi Indians. University of Pennsylvania Museum, *Anthropological Publications*, vol. 1, no. 2, Philadelphia, 1911, pp. 157–245.

184. SPENCE, LEWIS. *The Popul Vuh: The Mythic and Heroic Sagas of the Kichés of Central America*. London, 1908. 63 pp.

185. SPINDEN, HERBERT JOSEPH. American Indian Poetry. *Natural History*, vol. 19, 1919, pp. 301–308.

186. ——— *Songs of the Tewa:* with an essay on American Indian Poetry. New York, 1933. 125 pp.

187. SQUIER, E. G. Historical and Mythological Traditions of the Algonquins, with a translation of the Walum-Olum, or bark record of the Lenni Lenape. Paper read before New York Historical Society, June, 1848. Reprinted from *American Whig Review*, February, 1849, in *The Indian Miscellany*, ed. by W. W. Beach, Albany, 1877, pp. 2–42.

188. STEVENSON, (Mrs.) MATILDA COXE. The Sia. *11th Annual Report*, Bureau of American Ethnology, Washington, D. C., 1894, pp. 9–157.

189. ——— The Zuñi Indians. *23rd Annual Report*, Bureau of American Ethnology, Washington, D. C., 1904, pp. 1–608.

190. STRICKLEN, E. G. Notes on Eight Papago Songs. University of

California *Publications* in American Archaeology and Ethnology, vol. 20, 1923, pp. 361–366.

191. SWANTON, JOHN R. Haida Songs. *Publications* of American Ethnological Society, vol. 3, Leyden, Holland, 1912. v + 284 pp.

192. —— Religious Beliefs and Medical Practices of the Creek Indians. *42nd Annual Report*, Bureau of American Ethnology, Washington, D. C., 1928, pp. 473–672.

193. —— Social Organization and Social Usages of the Indians of the Creek Confederacy. *Ibid.*, pp. 23–472.

194. —— Tlingit Myths and Texts. *Bulletin 39*, Bureau of American Ethnology, Washington, D. C., 1909. viii + 451 pp.

195. THALBITZER, WILLIAM. The Ammassalik Eskimo: Part II, no. 3, *Language and Folklore*, Copenhagen, 1923.

196. —— *The Eskimo Language*. Copenhagen, 1904. xvii + 405 pp.

197. —— A Phonetical Study of the Eskimo Language. *Meddelelser om Gronland*, vol. 31, 1904.

198. TOZZER, ALFRED M. *A Comparative Study of the Mayas and Lacandones*. New York, 1907. Published for the Archaeological Institute of America. 189 pp.

199. TROYER, CARLOS. *Traditional Songs of the Zuñi Indians*. Philadelphia, 1913. 56 pp.

200. UNDERHILL, RUTH MURRAY. *Papago Indian Religion*. New York, 1946, 359 pp.

201. —— *Singing for Power*. Berkeley, Calif., 1938. 158 pp.

202. UNTERMEYER, LOUIS. Review of Cronyn, George: The Path on the Rainbow. *Dial*, vol. 66, March 8, 1919, pp. 240–241.

203. "VESTAL, STANLEY" (pseud. W. S. CAMPBELL). *Sitting Bull*. Boston and New York, 1932. xiv + 350 pp.

204. —— The Works of Sitting Bull, Real and Imaginary. In *Professional Writing*, by W. S. Campbell, New York, 1938, pp. 168–181.

205. VOTH, H. R. Oráibi Oáqöl Ceremony. Field Museum, *Anthropological Series*, vol. 6, no. 1, Chicago, 1903. 46 pp.

206. VOTH, H. R. and DORSEY, GEORGE A. The Oráibi Powamu Ceremony. Field Museum, *Anthropological Series*, vol. 3, no. 2, Chicago, 1901. 158 pp.

207. WALTON, E. L. and WATERMAN, T. T. American Indian Poetry. *American Anthropologist*, vol. 27, January, 1925, pp. 25–52.

208. WALTON, EDA LOU. Navajo Traditional Poetry: Its Content and Form. 2 vol. Ph. D. Dissertation, University of California, 1920.

209. ——— Navajo Verse Rhythms. *Poetry*, vol. 24, April, 1924, pp. 40–44.

WATERMAN, T. T. See WALTON.

WHEELWRIGHT, MARY C. See KLAH.

210. WISSLER, CLARK. *The American Indian*. 3rd ed., New York, 1938. xvii + 466 pp.

WYMAN, LELAND C. See KLUCKHOHN.

211. WYMAN, LELAND C. and KLUCKHOHN, CLYDE. Navaho Classification of Their Song Ceremonials. *Memoirs* of the American Anthropological Association, no. 50, 1938. 38 pp.

INDEX

INDEX